TONI
MORRISON

WOMEN OF ACHIEVEMENT

TONI MORRISON

Jean F. Blashfield

CHELSEA HOUSE PUBLISHERS
PHILADELPHIA

Frontispiece: Nobel Prize–winning novelist Toni Morrison lectures students at Purdue University in September 2000. Critics praise her lyrical prose and insights about the human condition.

PRODUCED BY 21st Century Publishing and Communications, Inc., New York, N.Y.

Chelsea House Publishers
EDITOR IN CHIEF Sally Cheney
ASSOCIATE EDITOR IN CHIEF Kim Shinners
PRODUCTION MANAGER Pamela Loos
ART DIRECTOR Sara Davis
DIRECTOR OF PHOTOGRAPHY Judy L. Hasday
COVER DESIGNER Keith Trego

The Chelsea House World Wide Web address is
http://www.chelseahouse.com

First Printing
1 3 5 7 9 8 6 4 2

Library of Congress Cataloging-in-Publication Data

Blashfield, Jean F.
Toni Morrison / Jean F. Blashfield.
    p. cm. — (Women of achievement)
Includes bibliographical references and index.
ISBN 0-7910-5885-9 (alk. paper) — ISBN 0-7910-5886-7 (pbk.: alk. paper)
1. Morrison, Toni—Juvenile literature. 2. Novelists, American—20th century—Biography—Juvenile literature. 3. Afro-American women novelists—Biography—Juvenile literature. [1. Morrison, Toni. 2. Authors, American. 3. Women—Biography. 4. Afro-Americans—Biography.] I. Title. II. Series.

PS3563.O8749 Z565 2000
813'.54—dc21
[B]   00-060135

CONTENTS

WOMEN of ACHIEVEMENT

Jane Addams
SOCIAL WORKER

Madeleine Albright
STATESWOMAN

Marian Anderson
SINGER

Susan B. Anthony
WOMAN SUFFRAGIST

Clara Barton
AMERICAN RED CROSS FOUNDER

Margaret Bourke-White
PHOTOGRAPHER

Rachel Carson
BIOLOGIST AND AUTHOR

Cher
SINGER AND ACTRESS

Hillary Rodham Clinton
FIRST LADY AND ATTORNEY

Katie Couric
JOURNALIST

Diana, Princess of Wales
HUMANITARIAN

Emily Dickinson
POET

Elizabeth Dole
POLITICIAN

Amelia Earhart
AVIATOR

Gloria Estefan
SINGER

Jodie Foster
ACTRESS AND DIRECTOR

Betty Friedan
FEMINIST

Althea Gibson
TENNIS CHAMPION

Ruth Bader Ginsburg
SUPREME COURT JUSTICE

Helen Hayes
ACTRESS

Katharine Hepburn
ACTRESS

Mahalia Jackson
GOSPEL SINGER

Helen Keller
HUMANITARIAN

**Ann Landers/
Abigail Van Buren**
COLUMNISTS

Barbara McClintock
BIOLOGIST

Margaret Mead
ANTHROPOLOGIST

Edna St. Vincent Millay
POET

Julia Morgan
ARCHITECT

Toni Morrison
AUTHOR

Grandma Moses
PAINTER

Lucretia Mott
WOMAN SUFFRAGIST

Sandra Day O'Connor
SUPREME COURT JUSTICE

Rosie O'Donnell
ENTERTAINER AND COMEDIAN

Georgia O'Keeffe
PAINTER

Eleanor Roosevelt
DIPLOMAT AND HUMANITARIAN

Wilma Rudolph
CHAMPION ATHLETE

Elizabeth Cady Stanton
WOMAN SUFFRAGIST

Harriet Beecher Stowe
AUTHOR AND ABOLITIONIST

Barbra Streisand
ENTERTAINER

Elizabeth Taylor
ACTRESS AND ACTIVIST

Mother Teresa
HUMANITARIAN AND
RELIGIOUS LEADER

Barbara Walters
JOURNALIST

Edith Wharton
AUTHOR

Phillis Wheatley
POET

Oprah Winfrey
ENTERTAINER

Babe Didrikson Zaharias
CHAMPION ATHLETE

"REMEMBER THE LADIES"

MATINA S. HORNER

"Remember the Ladies." That is what Abigail Adams wrote to her husband John, then a delegate to the Continental Congress, as the Founding Fathers met in Philadelphia to form a new nation in March of 1776. "Be more generous and favorable to them than your ancestors. Do not put such unlimited power in the hands of the Husbands. If particular care and attention is not paid to the Ladies," Abigail Adams warned, "we are determined to foment a Rebellion, and will not hold ourselves bound by any Laws in which we have no voice, or Representation."

The words of Abigail Adams, one of the earliest American advocates of women's rights, were prophetic. Because when we have not "remembered the ladies," they have, by their words and deeds, reminded us so forcefully of the omission that we cannot fail to remember them. For the history of American women is as interesting and varied as the history of our nation as a whole. American women have played an integral part in founding, settling, and building our country. Some we remember as remarkable women who—against great odds—achieved distinction in the public arena: Anne Hutchinson, who in the 17th century became a charismatic religious leader; Phillis Wheatley, an 18th-century black slave who became a poet; Susan B. Anthony, whose name is synonymous with the 19th-century women's rights movement, and who led the struggle to enfranchise women; and in the 20th century, Amelia Earhart, the first woman to cross the Atlantic Ocean by air.

These extraordinary women certainly merit our admiration, but other women, "common women," many of them all but forgotten, should also be recognized for their contributions to American thought and culture. Women have been community builders; they have founded schools and formed voluntary associations to help those in need; they have assumed the major responsibility for rearing children, passing on from one generation to the next the values that keep a culture alive. These and innumerable other contributions, once ignored, are now being recognized by scholars, students, and the public. It is exciting and gratifying that a part of our history that was hardly acknowledged a few generations ago is now being studied and brought to light.

In recent decades, the field of women's history has grown from obscurity to a politically controversial splinter movement to academic respectability, in many cases mainstreamed into such traditional disciplines as history, economics, and psychology. Scholars of women, both female and male, have organized research centers at such prestigious institutions as Wellesley College, Stanford University, and the University of California. Other notable centers for women's studies are the Center for the American Woman and Politics at the Eagleton Institute of Politics at Rutgers University; the Henry A. Murray Research Center for the Study of Lives, at Radcliffe College; and the Women's Research and Education Institute, the research arm of the Congressional Caucus on Women's Issues. Other scholars and public figures have established archives and libraries, such as the Schlesinger Library on the History of Women in America, at Radcliffe College, and the Sophia Smith Collection, at Smith College, to collect and preserve the written and tangible legacies of women.

From the initial donation of the Women's Rights Collection in 1943, the Schlesinger Library grew to encompass vast collections documenting the manifold accomplishments of American women. Simultaneously, the women's movement in general and the academic discipline of women's studies in particular also began with a narrow definition and gradually expanded their mandate. Early causes, such as woman suffrage and social reform, abolition, and organized labor were joined by newer concerns, such as the history of women in business and the professions and in politics and government; the study of the family; and social issues such as health policy and education.

Women, as historian Arthur M. Schlesinger, jr., once pointed out, "have constituted the most spectacular casualty of traditional history. They have made up at least half the human race, but you could never tell that by looking at the books historians write." The new breed of historians is remedying that omission. They have written books about immigrant women and about working-class women who struggled for survival in cities and about black women who met the challenges of life in rural areas. They are telling the stories of women who, despite the barriers of tradition and economics, became lawyers and doctors and public figures.

The women's studies movement has also led scholars to question traditional interpretations of their respective disciplines. For example, the study of war has traditionally been an exercise in military and political analysis, an examination of strategies planned and executed by men. But scholars of women's history have pointed out that wars have also been periods of tremendous change and even opportunity for women, because the very absence of men on the home front enabled them to expand their educational, economic, and professional activities and to assume leadership in their homes.

The early scholars of women's history showed a unique brand of courage in choosing to investigate new subjects and take new approaches to old ones. Often, like their subjects, they endured criticism and even ostracism by their academic colleagues. But their efforts have unquestionably been worthwhile, because with the publication of each new study and book another piece of the historical patchwork is sewn into place, revealing an increasingly comprehensive picture of the role of women in our rich and varied history.

Such books on groups of women are essential, but books that focus on the lives of individuals are equally indispensable. Biographies can be inspirational, offering their readers the example of people with vision who have looked outside themselves for their goals and have often struggled against great obstacles to achieve them. Marian Anderson, for instance, had to overcome racial bigotry in order to perfect her art and perform as a concert singer. Isadora Duncan defied the rules of classical dance to find true artistic freedom. Jane Addams had to break down society's notions of the proper role for women in order to create new social situations, notably the settlement house. All of these women had to come to terms both with themselves and with the world in which they lived. Only then could they move ahead as pioneers in their chosen callings.

Biography can inspire not only by adulation but also by realism. It helps us to see not only the qualities in others that we hope to emulate, but also, perhaps, the weaknesses that made them "human." By helping us identify with the subject on a more personal level they help us feel that we, too, can achieve such goals. We read about Eleanor Roosevelt, for instance, who occupied a unique and seemingly enviable position as the wife of the president. Yet we can sympathize with her inner dilemma; an inherently shy woman, she had to force herself to live a most public life in order to use her position to benefit others. We may not be able to imagine ourselves having the immense poetic talent of Emily Dickinson, but from her story we can understand the challenges faced by a creative woman who was expected to fulfill many family responsibilities. And though few of us will ever reach the level of athletic accomplishment displayed by Wilma Rudolph or Babe Zaharias, we can still appreciate their spirit, their overwhelming will to excel.

A biography is a multifaceted lens. It is first of all a magnification, the intimate examination of one particular life. But at the same time, it is a wide-angle lens, informing us about the world in which the subject lived. We come away from reading about one life knowing more about the social, political, and economic fabric of the time. It is for this reason, perhaps, that the great New England essayist Ralph Waldo Emerson wrote in 1841, "There is properly no history: only biography." And it is also why biography, and particularly women's biography, will continue to fascinate writers and readers alike.

Standing with Nobel Academy Secretary Sture Allén, Toni Morrison accepts the 1993 Nobel Prize for Literature, the highest honor the world can give a writer.

THE HIGHEST HONOR

Holding on to the arm of the King of Sweden, Carl XVI Gustaf, the elegant woman entered the Stockholm Concert Hall chamber to the applause of the world's elite. She was once young Chloe Wofford, raised in poverty in an industrial town in northern Ohio, but here in this beautiful chamber in Stockholm, Sweden, and to the rest of the world, she was famed writer Toni Morrison. The year was 1993 and she was here to receive the highest honor the world can give a writer, the Nobel Prize for Literature.

Dressed in a gorgeous, flowing gown designed for her by Bill Blass, the diminutive woman held her head high as she walked before the assembled crowd with pride and joy. The renowned writer had become only the eighth woman and the first African-American woman to win the literature prize, the most prestigious international writing award.

The Nobel Prize awards originated with Alfred Nobel, the Swedish chemist and industrialist who invented dynamite. Nobel's inventions made him quite wealthy, and when he died in

1896, he designated in his will the creation of five prizes, to be awarded in the fields of physics, chemistry, medicine or physiology, literature, and peace. (A sixth prize for economics was added in 1969.) The Nobel Prizes have been awarded annually since 1901, five years after his death.

The winner of the literature prize is determined by the Swedish Academy, an organization founded in 1786 to ensure the purity of the Swedish language. The academy did not function with any great consistency until after the death of Alfred Nobel, whose will gave it the task of administering the literature portion of the Nobel Prizes. Today the Swedish Academy consists of 18 members, all of whom are elected for life.

Each year the Nobel season begins in October when journalists from around the world gather in a room at the Stockholm Stock Exchange. There the journalists wait, buzzing and chattering, until, exactly at one o'clock, a clock strikes and the room's tall doors swing open. The permanent secretary of the Swedish Academy walks in to announce which world writer for that year best fulfills Alfred Nobel's call for "the most outstanding work in an ideal direction." In 1993, the name announced—Toni Morrison— astonished the literary world.

Most observers had expected the prize to go to someone who wrote in a language other than English, since for the past two years, the Nobel Prize for Literature had gone to English-speaking writers. Academy members seldom gave back-to-back awards to writers who used the same language. To do so for a third year was highly unusual. But the academy made the basis of its choice quite clear, praising Morrison's novels for their "American reality" and stating, "She delves into the language itself, a language she wants to liberate from the fetters of race. And she addresses us with the luster of poetry."

After the announcement of the prize winner, Sweden

issued a new postal stamp with Toni Morrison's picture on it. This was only the second time the country had produced a stamp honoring the winner of the Nobel Prize for Literature.

The Nobel Prize award ceremonies usually take place during the second week of December, and are accompanied by several days of festivities. Honorees attend speeches, receptions, lunches, dinners, and special concerts. They travel in chauffeur-driven limousines, drink champagne, and wear fancy gowns or white tie and tails.

In 1993, Nobel week swept Toni Morrison up into activities from December 6 to 10. On the Tuesday, December 7, she lunched at the American Embassy. Afterward Stockholm police escorted her to the Swedish Academy to deliver her Nobel Lecture in Literature.

Standing at the podium in front of a packed audience in the Academy's Grand Hall, the celebrated author began her speech with a story: "Once upon a time there was an old woman. Blind but wise." The tale gradually evolved into a meditation on language, as an entranced audience hung on her every word. The powerful language, with its moving metaphors and vivid descriptions, seized the imagination of every listener.

Morrison concluded her presentation with a statement on the importance of writing: "We die. That may be the meaning of life. But we do language. That may be the measure of our lives."

Two standing ovations greeted Toni Morrison's words. According to friend and critic John Leonard, the crowd consisted of "sons, sisters, nieces, cousins; editors, agents, critics; professors from Princeton, Harvard, and City College; well-wishers, witnesses, celebrants, pilgrims, support-groupies, friends."

During the next two days, every major publisher of Toni Morrison's books threw a reception to honor the author's accomplishments. On Thursday evening, she

Morrison's powerful writing has earned her much recognition. A special program dedicated to her, entitled "An Evening with Toni Morrison and Her Friends," was held at the Cathedral of St. John the Divine in New York City on April 5, 1994.

attended the grandest reception of the week, given by the Swedish Academy. And on Friday, December 10, Toni received her Nobel Prize at the beautiful, modern Stockholm Concert Hall.

How did young Chloe Wofford of Lorain, Ohio, come to stand on the stage of that great hall and receive the prestigious Nobel Prize in Literature? A private person, Toni Morrison has not revealed very much in interviews about her personal background and the choices she has made in life. A careful reading of her novels will not reveal many answers as she makes few direct autobiographical references in her stories.

But still, Morrison's writing contains many clues about where the author came from and the society that shaped her life, as well as the lives of many African Americans. As Paul Gray of *Time* magazine once observed, Toni's novels are "intensely imaginative responses to the specific historical and social pressures she has experienced as a black woman in the U.S. The imagination is all hers; the pressures have been the inheritance of millions."

Both of Toni Morrison's parents had migrated from the South in the early 1900s. Her mother's family had farmed the land there as sharecroppers, but they chose to head to the North, where there were more job opportunities.

2

A CHALLENGING CHILDHOOD

The woman who would come to be known as Toni Morrison was born on February 18, 1931, in Lorain, Ohio, a small steel-mill town just west of Cleveland. Her father, George Wofford—a shipyard welder—and her mother, Ramah Willis Wofford, named their second daughter Chloe Anthony Wofford. Soon Chloe had two younger brothers as well.

It wasn't easy being the second child out of four children, the famous author later recalled in an interview. "I was the one with the anonymous birth order," she explained. "There was my older sister, firstborn; me, void; my younger brother, first son; and another son, the family baby. Feeling left out, and trying to attract attention, I became the noisiest of them all."

Chloe was born into a family that was used to overcoming difficulties. Her mother, Ramah, had moved to Lorain at the age of six when the Willis family migrated north from Greenville, Alabama, in the early 1900s. In the South they had been sharecroppers—farmers who raised crops on someone else's land in exchange for a share of the harvest. The lives of sharecroppers were uncertain. They had no rights and could be thrown off the land at any time. The landowners controlled the seed supply as well as the equipment for measuring the harvest. Sharecroppers might end the growing season owing money to the owners instead of having made something to live on. And when a growing season went bad, sharecroppers were the first to suffer.

To make matters worse, the land on which the Willis family was sharecropping had once belonged to them. Chloe's great-grandmother was a Native American who had received 88 acres of land when the federal government divided reservation land into parcels after the Civil War. Although she couldn't read, she became a midwife, gaining a reputation that spread throughout Alabama. Over the years, the family piled up large debts and had to sell its cherished land to pay bills.

The desire for a better life loomed large in the dreams of the Willis family. Chloe's grandparents, Ardelia and John Solomon Willis, decided to move to the North when their older girls became teenagers. John left first, and soon obtained work in Kansas as a musician. Shortly afterward Ardelia Willis gathered all the cash she had—$18—packed up her seven children, and followed. She sent a note to her husband and told him to meet them in Kentucky, where John Willis soon found work in the coal mines. But the Willises never truly settled down in Kentucky because they wanted to live where their children could get a better education. They headed north again and ended up in Lorain, Ohio. Eventually, most members of the extended Willis family came north, too.

Chloe's father, George Wofford, had moved to Ohio from Georgia, eager to escape the South's violent racism. The Wofford family lived in Cartersville, Georgia, which is located on the edge of the Appalachian Mountains. Because the land there is too rocky and hilly for much agriculture, workers had to compete for jobs as laborers. Both African Americans and whites needed the work, but white men were usually hired first.

Nevertheless, John Wofford, George's father, had managed to work his way up to the position of locomotive operator with the Seaboard Railroad, driving a route from Cartersville to various cities in Alabama. The prestigious job allowed him to live comfortably among the middle-class white families, mostly European immigrants, though the Woffords were the only black family on an all-white street.

But then attitudes in Cartersville began to change. The economy slowed down and jobs became scarce. White men believed that black men threatened to take their jobs and so began to harass their rivals. Soon George's father lost his job. Tensions in the town ran high as white residents verbally abused the Woffords and even threw rocks at their house.

Someone accused Will Jackson, an African American whom George knew, of "insulting a white woman." In the early years of the 20th century, this charge was often brought against black men who had simply smiled at a white woman or said a polite "good morning." But the consequences were very serious. Mobs of violent white men made any excuse to vent their rage, often on young African-American males. Like many black victims of the period, Will Jackson was lynched—dragged by a vicious mob and then hanged. White men who committed such acts were seldom arrested or brought to trial. Many white southerners considered a lynching, in itself, an act of justice. During the early years of the 1900s, more than 1,100 black men were lynched, three of them in Cartersville, Georgia.

Determined to escape a fate like Will Jackson's, 16-year-old George Wofford and his brother Henry decided to leave Cartersville. They knew the North also held better employment opportunities and were confident they could succeed there. Like many other young African-American men during the 1910s and 1920s,

During the 1930s the National Association for the Advancement of Colored People took steps to end racial violence by investigating and publicizing lynchings, announcing such tragedies on flags displayed outside its New York City headquarters.

the two brothers headed off, seeking a better, safer life in the North. They settled in Lorain, Ohio.

The industrial city of Lorain sits on the edge of Lake Erie, about 26 miles west of Cleveland. The town serves as a center for the coal and iron-ore shipping industry throughout the Great Lakes. When George and Henry Wofford arrived, they joined many other African Americans who had found work in the city's mills and shipyards. George became an adept welder, often working on steel panels for ships.

George Wofford and Ramah Willis met in Lorain and later married in the 1920s. As they began their family, they faced a new challenge. In 1929 the U.S. economy collapsed, and the country had entered what came to be known as the Great Depression. Many people, including Chloe's father, lost their jobs. Financial problems plagued the Wofford family for most of Chloe's childhood, although her father would take any work he could find, often holding down three jobs at once. He did everything from washing cars to working on road construction sites in his effort to support his family. But like other African-American men, he often found himself at a disadvantage. White men were offered jobs first, and often no jobs were left for blacks.

Young Chloe Wofford watched her father struggle against racism. She would later note how she came to view Ohio as a microcosm representing nationwide racial issues. "The northern part of the state had underground railway stations and a history of black people escaping into Canada," she explained, "but the southern part of the state is as much Kentucky as there is, complete with cross burnings. Ohio is a curious juxtaposition of what was ideal in this country and what was base."

Chloe grew up knowing not just two Ohios but two disparate attitudes toward white people. Based on what he had seen and experienced, Chloe's father had developed a deep mistrust of white society. George Wofford wanted to live his own life and had no desire for equality with whites, believing that black people were superior. He refused to have anything to do with white people and would not let them in the house. White insurance agents and other salesmen learned to approach the Wofford family only when George was away.

In contrast, Ramah Wofford and the members of her extended family kept to their own, tight-knit black community, but they remained tolerant of white people. Chloe's mother felt confident that, in time, all races would get along, and she was going to do what she could to make that happen. In the meantime, though, Ramah took steps to protect her children from white oppression. On the Saturday afternoons that the children attended a matinee movie, she would go to the theater to check that they sat wherever they wanted, not in designated "colored" sections, where blacks were often forced to sit. Sometimes she went into the theater herself and sat among white people, making sure that since she had done it, anyone could.

When Ramah Wofford saw injustice, she believed in taking steps to set things right. During Chloe's early childhood, many families were struggling to make ends meet during the Great Depression. Chloe's family sometimes had to accept food from the U.S. government in order to eat. Once the government-relief flour they received was so old that it had maggots in it. Chloe's mother took pen in hand and wrote to President Franklin D. Roosevelt himself about the problem. "My mother believed something should be done about inhuman situations," Chloe later recalled.

If necessary, Ramah Wofford would also directly challenge authority. When Chloe and her sister Lois were little, they were exposed to tuberculosis, an infectious and often fatal lung disease for which there was no known cure. Doctors insisted that the two girls be placed in a tuberculosis hospital. But the girls' mother believed that no one who went into that hospital came out alive. She kept the girls at home, and they didn't come down with the disease, which may have happened if Chloe's mother had followed the doctors' orders.

In the early 1930s the young Wofford family lived in a small apartment over a store. They were eventually able to rent a small house. But times were hard. During the height of the Depression, George Wofford couldn't always find work and was sometimes unable to pay the $4-a-week rent.

When Chloe was about two years old, their white landlord tried to evict them from their house. Ramah simply tore the eviction notice off the front door, and the Woffords refused to leave. One night, when they were all asleep, someone set the house on fire. Fortunately no one was killed or injured, but the family and their friends assumed the landlord had set the blaze to force the Woffords out. As Chloe grew up, the story was retold over and over again, and the incident took on more racial significance, especially in her father's mind. The little girl learned from him to

keep a "constant vigilance and awareness" toward white people.

Chloe not only absorbed her parents' attitudes toward other people, but she also learned their stories. A favorite family activity was listening to the tales told by both parents, though the best ones came from her father. Besides retelling in terrifying detail the story of the landlord who tried to burn down their house, he spurred his children's imagination with tales of ghosts and supernatural beings—stories that have always been an important part of African-American history and folklore. After listening to their parents' stories, the Wofford children would then create their own to share as they began exploring the world of imagination.

Chloe's parents also educated their children about the accomplishments of many great African Americans, including scientists and inventors. They had designed airplanes, discovered electricity, and invented shoes. Chloe was confused to hear a black man had invented

Like the African-American men pictured here, Chloe's father, George Wofford, often waited for work during the Great Depression only to discover that jobs were not available.

Young Chloe's parents made sure she knew about African-American scientists and inventors such as Granville T. Woods (above). Woods left school at the age of 10 but went on to patent more than 35 electrical and mechanical inventions. He was known as the "Black Edison."

shoes, and exclaimed, "Oh, Mama, everybody in the world must have had sense enough to wrap his feet." "I am telling you," her mother replied, "a Negro invented shoes." Years later Chloe would verify her mother's words when she learned that a patent for the overshoe was indeed issued to a black man in the early 1900s.

The Wofford family also told and retold their dreams to one another, believing that each person's dreams had special meaning and significance. Grandmother Willis also studied Chloe's dreams to predict winning numbers in gambling and for a while had great luck. Ardelia Willis enjoyed playing the numbers game, in which the gambler chose a three-digit number and then placed a bet that that number would be drawn. Mrs. Willis had a book that she used to translate images from Chloe's dreams into numbers. For a time young Chloe enjoyed the special attention as her grandmother asked her to describe her dreams: "It was lovely to have magic that could turn into the pleasure of pleasing one's grandmother and that was also profitable," the acclaimed writer would later remember. "My dream life is still so real to me that I can hardly distinguish it from the other."

No matter what difficulties they faced, the members of the Wofford family also found pleasure in reading. Ramah Wofford had told Chloe and her siblings how not very long ago black people in the South had often been prevented from going to school. Some states made it illegal for black children to learn how to read. Any southern child who was lucky enough to go to school and learn to read would take that knowledge home and teach others. Chloe's grandfather John Solomon Willis never attended school, but he learned to read on his own.

Dreaming, reading, and storytelling all centered on language. As Chloe grew up, she absorbed two languages. One was the language of her larger community, which included whites, Latinos, and European immigrants.

Her parents made certain that Chloe and her sisters and brothers learned to use the language of that world. But George and Ramah Wofford also demonstrated that the language of the African-American people was, as their grown-up daughter would later recall, "powerful, vivid" and "worthy of being revered." She remembered how her parents spoke English in several different ways: "[W]hen something terribly important was to be said, it was highly sermonic, highly formalized, biblical in a sense, and easily so. [My parents] could move easily into the language of the King James Bible and then back to standard English, and then segue into language that we would call street."

Chloe particularly enjoyed learning about language by reading. From a very young age, she could usually be found caught up in some story. Because of her love of books, she was already reading when she started first grade in the integrated neighborhood school. The only African American in her class, she was also the only child who could read. Chloe's teachers often seated her with newly arrived immigrant children. She would read and talk to the children to help them learn the English language.

Reading and sharing knowledge wasn't always a happy experience, however. Years later she described the pain of being rejected because of her race. Once, when in fifth grade, Chloe sat next to a newly arrived immigrant child who spoke no English: "I read well, and I taught him to read just by doing it. I remember the moment he found out that I was black—a nigger. It took him six months; he was told. And that's the moment when he belonged, that was his entrance. Every immigrant knew he would not come at the very bottom. He had to come above at least one group— and that was us."

Chloe found solace and much pleasure in listening to and singing music. She especially enjoyed listening to her mother, who sang both spirituals and classical opera. Ramah Wofford's voice resounded at home and in churches throughout the greater Cleveland area. The Wofford family attended the Greater Saint Matthew A.M.E. (Methodist) Church in Lorain, where Chloe's mother regularly sang solos. Their lives centered around the church, which was the heart of their close-knit community, for as Chloe would later recall, "The society was there, the art was there, the politics were there, the theology was there, everything was there."

Chloe's mother wasn't the only musical person in the family. Grandfather Willis had, at one time, earned money playing the violin, although his music gigs forced him to leave the family for long periods of time. Before Chloe was born, her maternal grandmother had played the piano in theaters to accompany silent movies. Because early movies had no sound, the piano music communicated the film's mood to the audience, setting the tone, for example, as cheerful, romantic, or frightening. The rest of the Wofford family members showed great musical abilities as well. They could sing or play just about anything. Chloe would later describe the singing her family did as "kind of talking to oneself musically."

When the Great Depression ended and the family had more money, Chloe took music lessons and enrolled in dancing class. She dreamed of one day becoming a ballet dancer like the famous Native-American ballerina Maria Tallchief, who was at the time gaining fame with the New York City Ballet. At age 13, Chloe helped pay the family bills when she took a job after school as a part-time maid.

The Woffords' community in Lorain was a place where neighbors worked together to make sure the children behaved and learned the things they needed to know in order to succeed in life. Chloe later explained: "The racial and ethnic mix [in Lorain] was

so tight and so unhostile, and there were no black neighborhoods. . . . There were wealthy neighborhoods but all of the poor people, which we were—the workers—lived next door to each other. . . . We all shared the small space, one high school, three junior high schools, these totally dedicated teachers, poverty, and that kind of life."

Chloe found safety among African Americans, even the ones whom she knew were involved in "vaguely criminal" activities: "Men who gambled, sold illegal liquor, or what have you. But when we saw them on the street they were safety zones for us. If we needed to get home, they took us. If we were someplace where we shouldn't be, they told us. If we needed protection, they gave it. So I always felt surrounded by these black men who were safe. I knew I was safe with them."

Secure within her own black community, Chloe

A group of black women standing in front of their church in Ohio. The church provided a social center for the Woffords and for many other African Americans.

Senior class treasurer Chloe Wofford (left), poses with other class government officers. During high school, she also served as associate editor of the yearbook and participated in the drama club.

found herself gradually adopting her father's attitude of not trusting any white people.

But in Lorain Chloe was also absorbing the confidence that she had the ability to do anything she wanted. She never found poverty degrading. It was just a fact of life, one that was totally offset by her parents' ability to make their children recognize they were "extraordinary deserving people." When she was growing up, Chloe would always remind herself of what lay in her power: "Black people had some choices. They could say life is limited for you, make the best of it; there are certain things forbidden to you, and you

might as well know that now. Or they said all things are possible and don't let anybody tell you that you can't do something. I came from a family that said the latter."

Chloe's parents always expected a lot from her, and she met their high expectations. As a student at Lorain High School, the studious teenager received high marks and participated in numerous activities: she served on the student council, as senior class treasurer, as a school library aide, and as associate editor for the *Hi-Standard*, the school yearbook. Chloe also made time for music and the school drama club.

An academic success at Lorain High School, Chloe graduated with honors in 1949. But completing high school was only the beginning of her educational path.

The Lorain High School Student Council with Chloe Wofford (third from left, middle row).

Howard University in Washington, D.C., provided an academic setting that was quite different from what Toni had expected.

3

AN ACADEMIC WORLD

Chloe Wofford grew up knowing the importance of getting a job and earning a living. But her family gave her the courage to consider doing something most of her black girlfriends thought impossible—going to college. One of Chloe's uncles had attended college, but she became the first woman on either side of her family to do so.

To help pay for Chloe's college education, George Wofford worked three jobs and Ramah took a position as a restroom attendant. In the fall of 1949, the aspiring student left for Howard University, located in Washington, D.C.

In the late 1940s many people considered Howard University the finest black university in the country. Founded in 1867 by the U.S. Congress to provide higher education for newly freed slaves, the school contained a growing population at the time Chloe enrolled. Up until then all of its students had been black. But in the late 1940s many World War II veterans had the opportunity to go to college through a government program called the G.I. Bill, and schools everywhere were accepting extra

Howard students gather to talk on campus. Toni believed that most of her classmates were more interested in having a social life than in studying.

students. Some of Howard's new students were white.

Chloe found that people at Howard had difficulty pronouncing her name. For some reason, they persisted in pronouncing "Chloe" as simply "clo" instead of "clo-ee." She decided to use the nickname Toni, based on her middle name, Anthony, instead.

Toni Wofford had expected to find Howard "full of brilliant black students" who would challenge her and keep her on her intellectual toes. But the new arrival was dismayed to discover that most students seemed to be more interested in developing a social life than in studying. They talked about parties, clothes, and popular music—and the faculty seemed to endorse this attitude. Toni was amazed. "From birth to Howard, I had been required to show some discipline, exert some initiative, hold jobs . . . and solve problems," she would later tell an interviewer. "Howard required none of that. We were treated like defective kids on the one hand . . . and ladies of the night on the other."

The new student was also stunned to find that the mostly black university did not focus on African-American thought, language, or history. For the most part—and on this issue Howard was certainly not alone—the school did not offer such courses. Curriculum centered on the usual "dead white men," as famed European and American writers have been called. Toni majored in English with a minor in the classics, preparing to be a college professor.

The girl from Lorain, Ohio, paid little attention to the white world surrounding her in Washington, D.C. She concentrated on getting to know the black people at the university. "Thinking on it now I suppose I was backward," she later told an interviewer, "but I never longed for social integration with white people. . . . I was prey to the racism of my early years in Lorain where the only truly interesting people to me were the black people."

Although not yet considering a career as a writer, Toni was already thinking about the meaning of being black. In one literature course, she wanted to write a paper about the black characters who appear in Shakespeare's plays. Her professor considered such a topic inappropriate and made her choose one that he regarded more important. Years later in an interview for television, Toni explained her belief that real education for a black person is "unlearning" such white values and language. In much of her writing, she says, she hunts for ways to remove "the gaze of the educator who was white" and write instead with African-American values and language.

Most of the other students at Howard didn't seem to care about black values and culture. They thought Toni should not be so serious. They believed that college was about parties and good times.

Actually, Toni did not only study while at Howard.

She joined the black sorority Alpha Kappa Alpha, which had been founded at Howard University in 1908. It was the first Greek-letter society for African-American women and quickly evolved into a national organization.

Continuing an interest in drama that had started in high school, Toni joined the Howard University Players, the campus theater company. The freshman from Ohio was a welcome addition to many casts, especially in the Shakespearean plays. She later explained how, unlike most of her classes, the theater company was "a place where hard work, thought, and talent" were the most important assets a person could have.

Although Toni had made occasional visits to the South as a child, visiting extended family members, she learned a great deal more about the region when she and the Howard Players toured there. Each summer, the troupe traveled through southern states, putting on performances. Years later she described her reaction to the tour's predominately African-American audiences: "What impressed me was the sight of so many people like me, like my relatives. . . . What I was aware of primarily were the black people there, and they were like people in Lorain, Ohio. And I didn't have to change my language or my manners."

The members of the troupe traveled by car caravan. Sometimes the theater company didn't arrive on time to keep its hotel reservations. If that happened, the faculty members usually called a local black church and the minister or his wife would locate church members who were willing to provide housing for the players.

At times the cast performed in small towns where black people were not allowed to eat in the local restaurants. Then the word went out to the troupe members as to which families in town would provide a good meal. As a result the players got to know southern black people whom they otherwise might not have met.

In 1953 Toni Wofford graduated from Howard University with a bachelor of arts degree in English and

Toni (right) performs in a school production of Shakespeare's King Richard III. *As a member of the Howard University Players, Toni found "a place where hard work, thought, and talent" were essential for success.*

a minor in classics. Her mother came from Ohio to watch proudly as the young graduate accepted her diploma.

Toni had not changed her goal of wanting to be a college professor, and so she continued her studies. She had been accepted at the graduate school at Cornell University, a predominantly white institution in Ithaca, New York. When she arrived there, Toni found herself, for the first time in her life, surrounded by white faces. The coursework at Cornell also provided a much greater challenge to the young graduate student than Howard had. But these difficulties were offset by the joy of studying with people seriously interested in learning.

While at Cornell, Toni heard about the 1954 U.S. Supreme Court decision in *Brown v. Board of Education of Topeka*. The case was brought by the parents of an African-American girl in Kansas, and it challenged several state laws that had established "separate but equal" schools for black children. The court's ruling on behalf of the child meant that public schools all over the nation could no longer legally segregate black and white students.

Toni later acknowledged that she was opposed to integrating the public schools. She was certain that black children would lose many benefits in the process, especially the advantages of an education with a black focus. "I didn't know why the assumption was that black children were going to learn better if they were in the company of white children," she said.

Meanwhile, the graduate student continued to work at Cornell on her studies of white writers. For her master of arts degree in English, she wrote a thesis on the themes of alienation and suicide in the works of southern novelist William Faulkner and feminist novelist Virginia Woolf. Unsatisfied with the final result, she later downplayed the value of her master's thesis, describing its conclusions as "shaky."

But Toni loved the writings of Faulkner. She learned to overlook the parts of books by him and other southern writers that reflected racist attitudes in their society. She explained, "[Faulkner] seemed to me the only writer who took black people seriously. Which is not to say he was, or was not, a bigot."

After earning her master's degree in 1955, Toni became an English instructor at Texas Southern University (TSU) in Houston, Texas. TSU had been created by the Texas legislature seven years earlier as a black university. When the new teacher arrived, the school was still establishing itself and its educational approach. Toni was hired to teach freshman introductory literature courses.

Although Toni didn't find teaching freshman English very exciting, TSU interested her in another way. Unlike Howard University, where the black culture was neglected or minimized, Texas Southern focused on its black heritage and even celebrated Negro History Week. Students and faculty took pride in their race and in their black history. While at TSU, Toni began to realize that up until then the life she had experienced in her family had defined for her what it meant to be black. But black culture meant something much bigger, both for Toni and the United States.

When Toni arrived at TSU, the first milestones of the modern civil rights movement were taking place. In 1955, Rosa Parks, a black seamstress in Montgomery, Alabama, got on a bus after a hard day of work. She took a seat toward the back of the bus, in the row just behind the "whites only" section. When a white man boarded, the bus driver told the blacks in that row to give up their seats. Rosa Parks refused and she was arrested. In response the African Americans of Montgomery began a boycott, refusing to ride the Montgomery buses until the policy was changed. Out of the Montgomery protest emerged a new black leader who would become a leading force in the civil rights movement—Dr. Martin Luther King Jr.

Toni's exposure to the philosophical ideas behind the civil rights movement expanded in 1957 when she left TSU and returned to Washington, D.C., having taken a position as an instructor at her alma mater, Howard University. She taught classes in freshman composition and classic literature. Some of her students and acquaintances were joining the burgeoning civil rights movement, eager to bring down segregationist laws. Among these future leaders were poet Amiri Baraka (at that time called LeRoi Jones) and Andrew Young, who later worked with Martin Luther King Jr. and went on to become a national political figure.

One of Toni's students was Stokely Carmichael, a native of Trinidad, who began making a name for himself in the national civil rights movement while at Howard. The philosophy student joined the Congress of Racial Equality (CORE) in its protest activities aimed at eliminating segregation at southern restaurants and other public facilities. After graduation Carmichael became a leader of the Student Nonviolent Coordinating Committee (SNCC), which worked to register black voters throughout the South. He also became a Freedom Rider, a member of an

Toni Wofford graduated from Howard University in 1953 with a degree in English. This senior portrait of her appeared in the Howard Bison *yearbook.*

Andrew Young (left) was a student at Howard University when Toni returned there as an instructor. He later worked with Martin Luther King Jr. (right). Here the two men represent the Southern Christian Leadership Conference at a March 24, 1967, news conference.

interracial group that traveled through the South in the mid-1960s, trying to end the practice of segregation on buses and trains. Eventually Stokely Carmichael openly advocated "black power," arguing that it was appropriate for blacks to use any means necessary, including violence, to gain political power.

In 1958 Toni married Harold Morrison, an architecture student from Jamaica with a soft island accent and considerable talent and ambition. What he did not have was the ability to accept his wife's own ambitions and desires.

The images of marriage that Toni Morrison knew were based on the relationships of her parents and grandparents. These marriages involved friendship and an equal give-and-take. "I didn't find imbalance or unevenness in these relationships," she recalled. But in her own marriage things were out of balance, and Toni found it difficult to submit to a dominant man, whose attitude toward women derived from his own culture. "Women in Jamaica are very subservient in their marriages," she later observed during a discussion of the problems in her marriage. "I was a constant nuisance to [him]," she said. "He didn't need me making judgments about him, which I did. A lot."

When Toni became pregnant, she continued to teach at the university. In 1961 Harold "Ford" Morrison was born, but the birth did not bring his father and mother closer. The Morrison marriage continued to deteriorate.

Toni escaped into writing. "It was as though I had nothing left but my imagination," she explained in an autobiographical article for *Current Biography Yearbook*. "I had no will, no judgment, no perspective, no power, no authority, no self—just this brutal sense of irony, melancholy and a trembling respect for words. I wrote like someone with a dirty habit. Secretly. Compulsively. Slyly."

In 1962 Toni joined a writers group that met once a month. During each informal meeting, a member would read a sample of his or her writing, and the others would critique it. Their comments would help the writer understand which descriptions worked effectively and which didn't, what character elements did and didn't ring true, and how the impact on the reader differed from what the writer expected.

Eventually Toni faced a meeting where she knew it would be her turn to read, but she had nothing new to offer. She racked her brain for an idea, then remembered a conversation she once had with a little black girl in Lorain. Although a child herself at the time, Toni vividly remembered her friend—a little black girl who desperately wanted to have blue eyes. Toni sat down and wrote out a short story based on the unhappy brown-eyed child's impossible wish.

After fulfilling her commitment to the writing group by reading her sketch, the young writer tucked it away. Little did she dream how that quickly written story would eventually set her on a new and unexpected course.

A single mother providing for two boys, Toni Morrison discovered writing could be a powerful weapon in overcoming loneliness.

4

OVERCOMING
THE LONELINESS

During the summer of 1964, while pregnant with her second child, Toni Morrison took her three-year-old son on a trip to Europe. While traveling she made the decision that she could not remain married to Harold Morrison. After returning home, she resigned from her job at Howard University, started divorce proceedings, and moved back to her parents' home in Lorain, Ohio. Soon afterward she gave birth to another son, whom she named Slade Kevin.

One day that fall, Toni answered an advertisement for an editorial position with L. W. Singer, a textbook subsidiary of Random House Publishers. The company, based in Syracuse, New York, was looking for an associate editor to help develop textbooks that reflected the African-American heritage. Toni was hired.

In 1965 Toni moved her sons and her belongings to Syracuse, a city located halfway between Albany and Buffalo. The young black woman, who herself had served as a maid when she was a teenager, hired a housekeeper to care for the children while she worked.

Life became tough for the single mother. She had to deal with a new job and she needed to ensure her children were well taken care of. She was living in a strange city with no friends or family to support her. Whenever she began to doubt her ability, however, she would remember her grandmother Willis, who on her own had moved her seven children north. Then Toni would tell herself that what she was doing was not at all as hard as what her grandmother had done.

Work and motherhood left Toni little time or inclination to make new friends in Syracuse. After she came home from her job in the evening, she cooked dinner and played with her sons until it was their bedtime. Once they were asleep, she had time for herself. Then loneliness and restlessness would descend. She would ponder her marriage and divorce and feel lost—as if some important part of her had died. Years later Toni described her feelings at the time: "I was working hard at a job and trying to be this competent person. But the dead girl—and not only was that girl dead in my mind, I thought she was dead in everybody's mind, aside from my family and my father and my mother—that person didn't exist anywhere."

In these quiet evening hours Toni would write. She pulled out the story she had created for her writers group in Washington, D.C., and started to expand her simple tale about the little black girl who prayed for blue eyes. Gradually, as Toni became absorbed in the task and began to take great pleasure in her writing, the anguish and loneliness eased. She immersed herself in the characters of her novel, which she called *The Bluest Eye*.

The story drew on Toni's memory of a conversation with a childhood friend. The two young girls were discussing whether God existed. The friend emphatically declared that He did not, because she had prayed for two years to be given blue eyes and had never received them. Toni, who thought her friend beautiful just the way she was, believed the girl would have looked ugly if her wish had actually been fulfilled. It saddened Toni

that the child could not recognize her own beauty but instead sought to look like a white girl.

In her story, Toni later recalled, she had one main goal: "There was just one thing that I wanted to write about, which was the true devastation of racism on the most vulnerable, the most helpless unit in the society— a black female and a child. I wanted to write about what it was like to be the subject of racism."

She also wanted to create a book whose main character was a little black girl. Her story, she hoped, would be the kind of book that she had always wanted to read, one about "a kind of person that was never in literature anywhere, never taken seriously by anybody."

Toni Morrison set *The Bluest Eye* in Lorain, Ohio, in 1941, in the years when the Great Depression was ending. At that time many white people were beginning to find jobs again, but black people had made little progress. Even though Toni used the streets and houses that she remembered in Lorain as the settings for her

Toni chose her hometown of Lorain, Ohio, as the setting for her first novel, The Bluest Eye.

novel, she knew that what existed in her memory was not necessarily what was actually there. The author has said that *The Bluest Eye* is autobiographical only to the extent that the process of writing was a process of reclaiming herself. She had reached a point where she no longer had a personal identity. "I was somebody's parent, somebody's this, somebody's that," Morrison explained, "but there was no me in this world." Writing *The Bluest Eye* was a way of rediscovering herself.

In spite of her loneliness and doubts, Toni did excellent work as an editor, and after 18 months, she was offered a job at the Random House headquarters in New York City. This was a better position than the one in Syracuse and an awesome change for the young mother. Random House is one of the largest and most influential publishing houses in the world, and its editors can have a profound effect on what Americans read and discuss. With this promotion, Toni became the first black senior editor in the company's history.

The move to New York City in 1967 took a lot of courage. In an interview, Toni recalled that her Ohio family "was alarmed because they said I had no family here, meaning there was no one who felt responsible for me here." She had to promise her mother that if she couldn't find a community—some kind of support group of friend or associates—in a year, she would return to Ohio. Her mother relaxed a bit when an elderly distant cousin was located in the city. At least Chloe, as she still called Toni, had "family" in New York.

Along with her two sons, Toni moved into a house in Queens, a borough of New York. She commuted from there by subway into Manhattan each day to work. The boys attended the United Nations International School at first and then enrolled in the private Walden School. She set about getting comfortable in the big city, but that wasn't always easy.

At first Toni continued to edit Random House textbooks sold directly to schools, but soon she began

working in the trade books division, which produces books that are sold in bookstores. There Toni was given the task of increasing the number of black authors the company published.

At night the busy editor continued to work on her novel, *The Bluest Eye*. At first she wrote in a room closed off from the living room, where the boys would play. But because they interrupted her regularly with trivial matters, she realized they wanted her near them. So she moved her work into the living room and learned to tune out their noise. She later said, "I would always write under conditions that probably are unbearable when people think of how one writes."

In 1967 Toni and her sons moved from the small city of Syracuse to the massive metropolis of New York City. There the aspiring writer assumed the duties of senior editor for the trade book division of Random House Publishers.

When she finally finished the manuscript, Toni was dissatisfied. She wanted to change the focus, as well as the language, which she later described as "scholarly bombast." Toni found the rewriting process "thrilling to do. But if I had approached it like, 'Oh, my God, I did it *wrong*, now I have to do it right,' I would never have done it at all."

As the young writer worked she had to learn to trust her own instincts. At first, she thought that the new version didn't sound like writing should—it wasn't "writerly enough." But gradually, when phrases, sentences, and whole paragraphs remained unchanged during revision after revision, she began to trust that her ideas were sound.

Even in the big, busy city of New York, Toni did not have much of a social life. The time needed for writing—and rewriting—had become more important to her. While she was raising her children, working, and writing, she kept her world as simple as possible. One day, when her life had been particularly hectic, she decided to take stock of her responsibilities and desires. First, she compiled a list of things she needed to do, which ranged from being a good mother to taking care of the small necessities of daily life, such as calling the phone company. Then she concentrated on figuring out what items on the list were things she *wanted* to do. Only two goals made it to the final list: "two things without which I couldn't live: mother my children and write books." Everything else became unimportant extras.

There was room for little else in Toni's life—including romance. At one point, Toni had a long-term relationship with a man who asked her to marry him. She found the idea appealing because she genuinely enjoyed his company, but she declined his proposal when she realized that he wanted her to give up her work in New York and move elsewhere with him.

Toni has acknowledged that over time she came to completely distrust romance. "Women who would want it are precisely the kind of women I would never like to be," she once said. "I only know that I will never again trust my life, my future, to the whims of men, in companies or out. Never again will their judgment have anything to do with what I think I can do."

When the aspiring writer finished *The Bluest Eye*, she sent copies of the manuscript to various publishers. Concerned that her company would prefer she concentrate on editing Random House books—not writing her own—she did not tell anyone there that she had completed a novel.

The book was turned down by a number of publishing companies, but some editors who read it suggested changes. Toni did not want to change her story. In despair, she sent the manuscript off to yet another publisher and then put the book out of her mind. She spent many months feeling vaguely sad. It wasn't until she had developed an idea for another novel that she realized the source of her sorrow: she had finished the story of the people she had come to love, and she missed having those fictional characters in her life.

Toni began to think about an idea for a new book that would feature a woman who was totally unconventional. That character would contrast with another woman whose personality was the complete opposite. Toni was writing again, and the idea of publishing her first novel no longer occupied her thoughts. As she explained, it no longer mattered: "If all the publishers had disappeared in one night, I would have written anyway."

After she had become absorbed in writing her second novel, Toni was thrilled to learn that *The Bluest Eye* had been accepted for publication by Holt, Rinehart, and Winston. Life became incredibly busy as over the following months, she edited during the day, worked on writing her next novel at night, and managed to fit the time in to read and make corrections to the proofs of her first novel before it went to press. However, she neglected to tell her editor at Holt that she wanted to use her original name, Chloe Wofford, on the book. When *The Bluest Eye* was published in 1970, its author was listed as Toni Morrison.

The book intrigued readers with its very first sentences. *The Bluest Eye* starts out sounding like part of the white world of the Dick-and-Jane books usually used to teach reading from the 1930s through the 1960s:

> *Here is the house. It is green and white. It has a red door.*
> *It is very pretty. Here is the family. Mother, Father, Dick,*
> *and Jane live in the green-and-white house. They are very*
> *happy. See Jane. She has a red dress. She wants to play.*
> *Who will play with Jane? See the cat. It goes meow-meow.*
> *Come and play. Come play with Jane.*

The pretty green-and-white house is not that of Toni's family. Nor is it the house of Pecola Breedlove, the central character in *The Bluest Eye*. Pecola, a very dark-skinned black girl, feels ugly in the 1930s white society in which she lives. She is certain that if she had the blue eyes so admired by her society, life would be wonderful. With blue eyes, Pecola believes, she would enter the Dick-and-Jane world. But of course, her dream never comes true. Instead, the vast gap between what is and what she wishes for drives Pecola mad.

The Bluest Eye received mixed reviews, although the fact that the novel was reviewed at all was a good sign. Critic John Leonard praised the book in the *New York Times,* saying, "Morrison expresses the negative of the Dick-and-Jane-and-Mother-and-Father-and-Dog-and-Cat photograph that appears in our reading primers, and she does it with a prose so precise, so faithful to speech, and so charged with pain and wonder that the novel becomes poetry." He added that the writing was not just poetry but "also history, sociology, folklore, nightmare, and music."

Remembering the events from the publication of *The Bluest Eye,* Toni later recalled, "I did not think that it would be widely distributed because it was about things that probably nobody was interested in except me. I was interested in reading a kind of book that I had never read before." She was right—the book sold only about 2,000 copies in its original hardbound edition.

Although the sales of Toni's first novel were small, its impact was immense. *The Bluest Eye* soon inspired many other African-American woman writers. Bebe Moore Campbell, author of *Brothers and Sisters*, as well as Gloria Naylor, whose first book was *The Women of Brewster Place*, have both remarked that Morrison's novel inspired them to write themselves. "I had all the permission I needed to become a writer—someone who looked like me had written a masterpiece," said Campbell.

Gloria Naylor recalled that *The Bluest Eye* made a strong impression on her:

Morrison's The Bluest Eye *inspired many African-American women writers, including Gloria Naylor, author of* The Women of Brewster Place.

> [The book] served two vital purposes at that moment in my life. It said to a young poet, struggling to break into prose, that the barriers were flexible; at the core of it all is language, and if you're skilled enough with that, you can create your own genre. And it said to a young black woman, struggling to find a mirror of her worth in this society, not only is your story worth telling but it can be told in words so painstakingly eloquent that it becomes a song.

Unaware of the effect her book was having on others and very conscious of her responsibility to provide for her two sons, Toni made no plans to leave her day job. And work was going well. One of her projects at Random House was a compilation by Middleton (Spike) Harris covering 300 years of black history. Toni was editing numerous newspaper clippings, photos, slave sales sheets, music, recipes, dream interpretations, and other items for the historical album, entitled *The Black Book*. The purpose of *The Black Book*, Morrison

NEGROES, NEGROES.

The undersigned has just arrived in Lumpkin from Virginia, with a likely lot of negroes, about 40 in number, embracing every shade and variety. He has seamstresses, chamber maids, field hands, and doubts not that he is able to fill the bill of any who may want to buy. He has sold over two hundred negroes in this section, mostly in this county, and flatters himself that he has so far given satisfaction to his purchasers. Being a regular trader to this market he has nothing to gain by misrepresentation, and will, therefore, warrant every negro sold to come up to the bill, squarely and completely. Give him a call at his Mart.

J. F. MOSES.
Lumpkin, Ga., Nov. 14th, 1859.

During the editing of The Black Book, *Toni reviewed countless items for inclusion, including posters such as this 1859 advertisement of a slave sale.*

explained, was to bring to life the "people who had always been viewed only as percentages."

Toni reviewed countless items for possible inclusion in the project, among them an old book of dream interpretation. Dreams of people of color, it said, would bring riches and health to the dreamer. Toni referred to this notion in her description of *The Black Book:* "With the whole world as its couch and white America as its pillow, it dreams of colored people. It is indeed an excellent dream."

While preparing *The Black Book* for publication, Toni discovered a newspaper clipping about a slave who had escaped to the North. When slave-catchers found her, she killed her own children rather than have them suffer in slavery as she had done. This story haunted Toni for years.

Published in 1974, *The Black Book* received enthusiastic reviews. In *Ms* magazine Dorothy Eugenia Robinson praised the historical album for exposing African Americans to

the pain and pride of rediscovering the collective black experience. It is finding the essence of ourselves and holding on. *The Black Book* is a kind of scrapbook of patiently assembled samples of black history and culture. What has evolved is a pictorial folk journey of black people, places, events, handcrafts, inventions, songs, and folklore. . . . *The Black Book* informs, disturbs, maybe even shocks. It unsettles complacency and demands confrontation with raw reality. It is by no means an easy book to experience, but it's a necessary one.

Reviewer Marilyn Sanders Mobley noted that *The Black Book* was Toni Morrison's "own meditation on history" in which one can "find many of the historical roots that work their way into Morrison's fiction, for central to her representations of African American life and culture is history, particularly the question of how history has shaped our identity and vice versa."

Toni Morrison published an essay in the *New York Times Magazine* entitled "Rediscovering Black History," in which she discussed *The Black Book*. She explained that the project was in part a response to what she viewed as a disturbing trend among some African Americans as an outgrowth of Black Power and the slogan "Black Is Beautiful":

> When the strength of a people rests on its beauty, when the focus is on how one looks rather than what one is, we are in trouble. When we are urged to confuse dignity with prettiness, and presence with image, we are being distracted from what *is* worthy about us: for example, our intelligence, our resilience, our skill, our tenacity, irony or spiritual health. And in that absolute fit of reacting to white values, we may very well have removed the patient's heart in order to improve his complexion.

She went on to say that *The Black Book* was designed to make African Americans aware of their history and of the great things they had accomplished.

Although Toni found her work projects stimulating, she was also busy expanding her activities. In 1971 she had returned to teaching at the university level for the first time since leaving Howard. Morrison became an associate professor of English, teaching part-time at the State University of New York at Purchase, located north of New York City.

As Toni edited books and read more widely in American and world literature, she was disturbed by the conspicuous absence of female characters. The novels contained no women like those she had known growing up, strong black women who were complete and complex characters. She decided to answer that absence in her own writing. *Sula* is set in a nonexistent northern Ohio town named Medallion. It is a story of a lifelong friendship between two very different women. Sula Peace and Nell Wright become best friends when they are 12 years old, but when they grow up, Sula leaves town, roaming from city to city for 10 years. When she returns to her hometown, Sula discovers that her friend Nell is immersed in a conventional life and is no longer able to understand her. In fact, no one in town understands Sula. She scares them, and they label her "evil." They begin to connect tragic events with Sula's presence. Both Sula and Nell learn to accept the consequences of their choices. In *Sula,* Toni Morrison explores the nature of friendship and the power of reconciliation.

Reviewer Claudia Tate described the character of Sula as first "simply unusual, then outrageous, and eventually evil. She becomes a pariah of her community, a measuring stick of what's evil and, ironically, inspires goodness in those around her."

The negative attitudes of the townspeople toward Sula were deeply rooted in superstition. Toni sees superstition as a fundamental part of the lives of black people and has admitted that she herself is superstitious. She once told an interviewer, "Whatever it is that I am has something to do with my relationship to things other than human beings. In *Sula* the people are like the people I have always known," and whose "relationship to evil is what preoccupied me throughout the book."

Published in 1973 by Alfred Knopf (a division of Random House), *Sula* received more notice than *The Bluest Eye*. Reviewers responded positively to Toni's deft handling of language and the virtual poetry of her writing. In 1975 the novel was nominated for a National Book Award, an honor awarded annually by U.S. book

publishers to recognize fine literature. *Sula* was also chosen as an alternative selection of the Book-of-the-Month Club. Clearly, an important new writer had appeared on the scene.

But Toni didn't yet have the courage to call herself a "writer." She usually identified herself as a mother who happened to write or as an editor who was fortunate enough to have a couple of her own books published.

The Bluest Eye and *Sula* made Toni Morrison a favorite of literary interviewers. She spoke with authority, insight, and humor on African-American literature, black-white relations, language, and society in general. However, she made a policy not to reveal much personal information about herself and her

The critical success of The Bluest Eye *and* Sula *established Toni Morrison (right) as an important American writer. Her newfound celebrity brought numerous invitations, such as this author luncheon with Lillian Carter, mother of President Jimmy Carter, in 1977.*

Toni hugs her younger son, Slade, outside their home in upstate New York. As adults, Slade and his older brother, Ford, would admit that it was difficult having a mother who was a writer.

background. "My personal life is most unexciting," she explained, "and I like it like that."

As the author of two positively reviewed novels, Toni began to be asked to give public readings. Her first reading, in 1974, was given in the back room of a Harlem bookstore. One observer described the presentation: "She talks for a while, lectures in a casual, self-assured way, then drops her voice, almost whispers, takes up the honeyed cadences that make her readings among the most effective of any writer's living today."

The author who takes such pride in the language of her books loves to read them aloud. "It is the thing that black people love so much—the saying of words, holding them on the tongue, experimenting with them, playing with them," Morrison says. "It's a love, a passion."

With the financial success of *Sula*, Toni could afford to buy a house some distance from Manhattan, in Rockland County, New York. She faced a 45-minute commute twice a day, but she found the inconvenience worth the benefits of raising her boys in the suburbs and enjoying her newest hobby, gardening. At first, Ford and Slade continued to go to their school in Manhattan, but they later attended the local public school.

As adults, the children of Toni Morrison admitted that it was difficult having a mother who wrote novels. It is hard for writers to focus on their families since they're in the world that exists in their mind—a world they hope to translate to paper. When Toni was immersed in writing a book, she couldn't give the boys her full attention. However, she could never get away with saying, "Leave me alone, I'm writing." She knew that such a request "doesn't mean anything to a child. What they deserve and need, in-house, is a mother. They do not need and cannot use a writer."

But the mother of the two boys was indeed a writer, a fact she now recognized. After *Sula* was published, her editor told her, "This is what you are going to be when you grow up. . . . This is what you are."

Toni thoroughly enjoyed editing books and saw her position at Random House as an important opportunity to nurture young black writers.

5

A CALL FOR BLACK WRITERS

Much as Toni Morrison loved writing, she also enjoyed editing. As the first black editor at Random House, she had the responsibility of encouraging African-American writers and providing a place for them in contemporary literature.

Toni's work as an editor during the 1970s and 1980s helped shape the African-American literary scene. Among the black writers she brought to public attention was Leon Forrest, sometimes called the "bard of black Chicago," whom she discovered. Morrison edited Forrest's first novel, *There is a Tree More Ancient Than Eden*, published in 1973 with a foreword by prominent black author Ralph Ellison. Toni edited Forrest's next two books as well.

In 1975 Toni edited *Corregidora*, a work by Gayl Jones. The novel earned high praise from noted authors Maya Angelou, James Baldwin, and John Updike. In the late 1970s, the influential editor also encouraged Toni Cade Bambara, a native of New York City's Harlem, to write. Bambara published two volumes of short stories and one novel before turning her focus to filmmaking. Together Toni Morrison, Gayl Jones, and Toni Cade Bambara are regarded as the three writers who opened up the publishing field to African-American women.

Not all the books Toni Morrison edited were fiction. Among the nonfiction books she helped prepare for publication was an autobiography of boxing great Muhammad Ali. His story was not simply of a young man determined to become heavyweight champion of the world. The controversial fighter, who at age 21 converted to Islam and changed his name from Cassius Clay, had refused on religious grounds to fight in the Vietnam War. As a result he had been suspended from boxing for four years. Because he stood up for his beliefs, Ali became a hero to many African Americans. After several years Ali worked his way back into the good graces of white sports fans. He eventually captured the heavyweight title an unprecedented three times over a period of 20 years.

Toni is proud of Ali's autobiography, *Muhammad Ali: The Greatest*. "It is beautiful. It is also massive," she recalled, laughing. "It was almost like editing the Bible and every comma became a thesis."

Another autobiography Toni worked on was that of black activist Angela Davis. A lecturer in philosophy at the University of California in Los Angeles in 1970, Davis was removed from her teaching position because of her radical political views. A Communist, she became involved in an attempted jail break from a Marin County jail, during which several people were killed. Davis was placed on the FBI's Most Wanted List and eventually charged with murder, kidnapping, and conspiracy. After a long, controversial trial that was closely covered, Davis was acquitted of all charges. She told her story in *Angela Davis: With My Mind on Freedom*, published in 1974.

Although working as a senior editor at Random House, Toni did not neglect her own writing. She thought about story ideas on the way to and from work, while washing dishes, and even while mowing the lawn. Then in the evenings, when she sat down to write, her

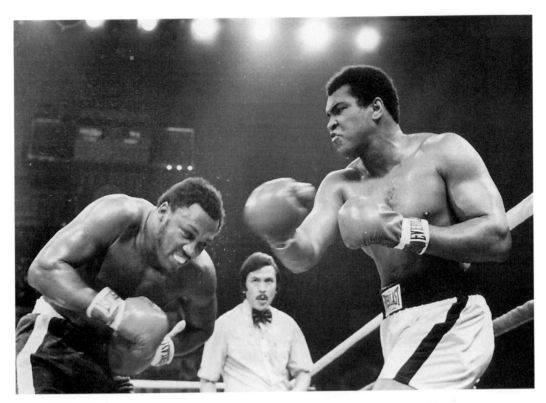

words flowed. Capturing the right expressions wasn't always easy, though. "If I don't feel the stride I can't do it," she once explained. "But once I get the hook, the right metaphor for a scene, I'm all right."

Morrison also continued teaching. She marked a further advancement in her career in 1976, when she became a visiting lecturer at Yale University in New Haven, Connecticut.

But then, in the midst of her professional success, Toni faced a great loss. Her father, George Wofford, died soon after the publication of *Sula*. She honored his memory by dedicating her next book, *Song of Solomon*, to "Daddy," who had always told her that she could do anything she set her mind to.

The Bluest Eye and *Sula* were intimate stories about women, whereas *Song of Solomon* put men on center stage in a broad, saga-like tale of a man's quest for his

Toni took great pride in her editing of boxer Muhammad Ali's autobiography. Here Ali (right) pounds Joe Frazier during a 1970s match.

Black activist Angela Davis also benefitted from Toni's editorial advice in the auto-biography Angela Davis: With My Mind on Freedom.

family heritage. "I could not create the same kind of enclosed world that I had in previous books," Toni explained. "Before it was as if I went into a room and shut the door in my books. I tried to pull the reader into that room. . . . It's a feminine concept—things happening in a room, a house."

According to Morrison, men travel, and may in fact even fly. *Song of Solomon* opens in Michigan, with a scene in which an insurance agent promises to fly across Lake Superior. "Flying is the central metaphor in 'Song'— the literal taking off and flying into the air, which is everybody's dream," Toni later explained. "My children used to talk about it all the time—they were amazed when they found they couldn't fly. They took it for granted that all they had to do was jump up and flap their arms."

The idea of men being able to fly—literally or metaphorically—she told an interviewer, is:

a part of black life, a positive, majestic thing, but there is a price to pay—the price is the children. The fathers may soar, they may triumph, they may leave, but the children know who they are; they remember, half in glory, and half in accusation. That is one of the points of "Song": all the men have left someone, and it is the children who remember it, sing about it, mythologize it, make it a part of their family history.

Song of Solomon introduced some of Toni's most memorable characters and their equally memorable names. Among them is Macon Dead III, known as Milkman, who travels from Michigan to the South in search of a rumored family treasure. His aunt, Pilate, who was born without a navel, and Milkman's sister, First Corinthians, got their names from words picked out of the Bible by their parents.

Milkman Dead is Toni's first fully developed male character. Previous male characters had lacked depth. As she later explained, she found the exercise of writing from the male point of view fascinating:

> I've never considered looking at the world and looking at women through the eyes of men. . . . I was obsessed by it . . . I mean trying to feel things that are of no interest to me but I think are of interest to men, like winning, like kicking somebody, like running toward a confrontation; that level of excitement when they are in danger.

By her third novel, Toni had already developed a pattern of leaving her books somewhat open-ended. The novels did not give complete closure to the action by implying that "[the characters] lived happily ever after" or "they survived that hard time, but more are on the way." Morrison prefers that "the reader . . . participate in this debate, in this dialogue," so she doesn't "tie all the knots." Toni considers stories that close completely, leaving "no echoes," as entertainment, not works of creativity.

Song of Solomon follows this pattern of letting readers decide for themselves what might happen next. "The end is unresolved," critic Reynolds Price comments in his review of the book. "Does Milkman survive to use his new knowledge, or does he die at the hands of a hateful friend? The hint is that he lives—in which case Toni Morrison has her next novel ready and waiting."

But Toni has never yet attached one of her novels to another. Each book explores new territory. What they have in common is her interest in the past. "What we [blacks] have to do is reintroduce ourselves to ourselves," she has said. "We have to know the past so that we can use it for now."

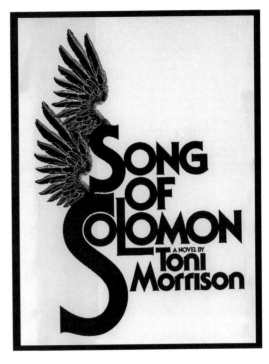

Released after the death of Toni's father, Song of Solomon, *Morrison's third novel, contains a dedication to "Daddy."*

In 1977 *Song of Solomon* became the first black-authored book chosen by the Book-of-the-Month Club as its main selection since Richard Wright's *Native Son*, published in 1940. *Song* also won the National Book Critics Circle Award, an honor voted on by almost 700 book reviewers.

Family routines at the Morrison home changed after the successful release of *Song of Solomon*. Although Toni had taken her children to Ohio every previous summer, that year she decided to stay in New York. As a widely known public figure, she was concerned that family and friends would treat her differently: "I didn't want those people [in Ohio] to look at me funny. I didn't want to experience myself as separate from them. I couldn't bear the fact that old ladies who used to tell me, 'Chloe, cross your legs' would look at me in any other way than that they had the right to tell me that still."

Those feelings were only reinforced the following year when the PBS television series *Writers in America* devoted an entire segment to exploring Toni Morrison's writing.

The success of *Song of Solomon* allowed the Morrison family to live more comfortably than before. Toni bought a converted boathouse fronting the Hudson River near Nyack, New York. Although from the street, the building appeared to be rather small and nondescript, the house stood a spacious four stories high. Toni also kept an apartment in New York City to use on days when activities there kept her busy.

Morrison decided that she no longer needed to work full-time and that she could, in fact, earn a living as a writer. She didn't quit working completely, however. She continued to teach part-time, write part-time, and edit four or five books a year for Random House.

As an instructor at several universities, Toni usually taught editing and writing. She shared with her students the unedited manuscripts that passed over her desk at Random House, as well as edited manuscripts that she thought could be improved. She would have students identify places where the author could have done a better job and point out why characters seemed unrealistic, dialogue sounded stilted, and settings appeared phony. Toni would caution her students to not make too many changes when editing—to not replace the author's style and words with their own.

As her students went through the process of learning how to improve and clarify a manuscript, Morrison stressed that they should apply what they learned to their own writing. Toni believed that too many people—her students included—want to be published authors before they are truly writers.

Toni's advice to aspiring authors begins with telling them to read. Writing, she has said, is "like any other craft. You have to know the industry and know what has been done. And then when you read and find something you like, try to figure out why you like it, what they did, and that's how you develop your craft. Not imitation, not even emulation, but just this wide range of reading."

In 1981, Morrison's fourth novel, *Tar Baby,* was published. The title of the book is associated with the Uncle Remus story of Br'er Rabbit and the Tar Baby. In that folktale, Br'er Fox plots to catch Br'er Rabbit by putting a baby made out of tar and turpentine at the side of the road. Br'er Rabbit comes along and becomes very upset when the Tar Baby doesn't speak to him. Eventually Br'er Rabbit hits the Tar Baby and becomes hopelessly entangled in the sticky tar.

Young Chloe Wofford had learned a slightly different version of this story from her mother in which a white man used Tar Baby to catch a rabbit. Something about the story frightened the little girl, and when she considered the story as an adult, she saw Tar Baby as a black woman and the rabbit who gets stuck in the tar as a black man. She used that image as the basis for *Tar Baby*.

In this novel Toni included white characters for the

first time. She also chose a setting that was not in the U.S. Midwest, but on a Caribbean island. The main character of *Tar Baby*, Jadine Childs, is the daughter of a white family's servants. Jadine is a black high-fashion model, leading a life that is totally foreign to traditional African-American women. As the story begins, all the characters are on the island and preparing for Christmas, when a black fugitive named Son appears. Jadine, though she yearns to belong to a white world, falls in love with Son, who wants to know and understand his black roots. Jadine runs off to New York City with Son, but the young couple soon faces insurmountable obstacles. She refuses to become part of his black world, and he cannot adapt to her white world. Son becomes the rabbit caught by the Tar Baby, Jadine.

A month after its publication, *Tar Baby* had leaped onto the best-seller lists. Morrison made a 14-city publicity tour for *Tar Baby,* with many television, radio, and newspaper interviews. Around the same time *Newsweek* magazine invited Toni Morrison to appear on its cover, a recognition never before given to either a black writer or an African-American woman. On hearing the news, she laughed and said, "The day you put a middle-aged, gray-haired colored lady on the magazine, I will know the revolution is over!"

The now well-known author received another honor in 1981 when she was elected to the American Academy and Institute of Arts and Letters. Membership to the academy is limited to 250 U.S. citizens, and it includes people noted for their achievements in art, literature, and music.

In the following months, Toni tried her hand at writing the lyrics for a musical called *New Orleans.* The show tells about a notorious section of 1917 New Orleans called Storyville. It was produced in 1983 at a workshop theater in New York.

By 1984, having published four novels that had

achieved fame and recognition, Toni Morrison decided to resign from Random House. She finally felt free to leave the world of regular work hours and regular paychecks to concentrate her efforts on the things she loved to do most—write and teach. In an interview discussing this decision, she wondered whether in the course of her editorial career she could have done more to bolster the commercial success of other black women writers. Rarely had their work sold as well as her books, a situation she regrets: "When I publish Toni Cade Bambara, when I publish Gayl Jones, if they would do what my own books have done [in sales], then I would feel really fantastic about it." But,

March 30, 1981 / $1.25

Newsweek

Black Magic

Novelist Toni Morrison

In March 1981, Toni Morrison became the first black writer and first African-American woman to appear on the cover of Newsweek *magazine.*

she observed, the "marketplace receives only one or two blacks in days when it's not fashionable. That's true of literature in general, but it's particularly true for Black writing."

However, Marilyn Sanders Mobley, a writer for *Southern Review,* insists that Toni proved instrumental as an editor: "She demonstrated that a black presence in high places—at least in publishing—could make a distinct difference. By the time she left Random House to devote her time and energies to her writing, she had . . . made places for other black writers."

In her play Dreaming Emmett *and her fifth novel,* Beloved, *Toni examines issues ranging from racial injustice to slavery.*

6

TRIBUTES TO
A PAINFUL PAST

When Toni Morrison left her long-time position at Random House in 1984, she didn't plan to write full-time. She accepted the Albert Schweitzer Chair in the Humanities at the State University of New York (SUNY) at Albany. This teaching position is a great honor for a professor to receive.

Because Albany is about 130 miles from Nyack, Toni arranged her schedule so that she taught there only a couple days a week. The rest of the time she worked at home. She found the change in routine took some getting used to: "[The situation was] a little odd. I hadn't been home at that time of day for years. I didn't know what the mailman looked like, and the house had entirely different sounds. . . . It was startling, and I didn't work at all."

In addition to teaching, Toni occasionally lectured and served as an instructor at writing workshops. Charles Ruas, who interviewed Toni after the publication of *Tar Baby,* described the author's style of presentation:

[Toni Morrison] is an impressive, strong woman, with an open countenance and a sonorous, melodious voice. Her eyes are amber-colored, of changing golden hue, and her face is extremely expressive, with sudden shifts in tone and mood. Her sense of humor is dominant, and she mimics in expression and voice the different people and characters in her conversation. But when she is deep in thought, her eyes almost closed, her voice grows quieter and quieter, lowering almost to a whisper, and the quality of her conversation approaches that incantatory flow which is akin to the lyric moments of her written style.

While in Albany, Morrison began work on her first play. SUNY's New York State Writers Institute commissioned Toni to create a play to commemorate the first federal holiday Martin Luther King Day. In thinking on the subject of civil rights for African Americans, the tragic story of Emmett Till came to her mind.

During the summer of 1955, Emmett Till, a 14-year-old African American, had traveled from Chicago to Mississippi, to visit relatives. There he befriended some local boys. Emmett showed them a photograph of a white girl, claiming she was his girlfriend. But they doubted his story and told him to prove it. If he was so friendly with a white girl, they said, he should go into the nearby grocery store and ask the white girl at the counter for a date. Emmett entered the store and chatted for a few minutes with the white cashier, who was the young wife of the store owner. As he was leaving, he was heard to say, "Bye, baby." A week later, Till was dead. His grotesquely beaten and nude body was found in the river with a bullet in the head and barbed wire around his neck.

Police arrested the store owner, Ron Bryant, and his brother-in-law, J. W. Milam, for the murder, and the case went to trial. A witness testified seeing the two men drag young Emmett into their truck and drive off with him. But the all-white male jury deliberated less

than an hour before finding the two men not guilty. The story plainly illustrated how the U.S. judicial system failed to preserve the rights of African Americans.

Although Toni seldom uses anything directly from real life in her fiction, she used Emmett Till's story as the inspiration for *Dreaming Emmett*. However, in her version, the 14-year-old boy comes back from death and tells the story of his murder in his own words. The play premiered on January 4, 1986, at the Marketplace Theater in Albany, New York.

At the same time Toni was also working hard on another novel. Since 1971, when she had edited

Toni loves engaging students' minds in classroom discussions. Here she chats with students at SUNY Albany, where she accepted the Albert Schweitzer Chair in the Humanities in 1984.

materials for *The Black Book*, one story she read had refused to leave her mind. The article, entitled "A Visit to the Slave Mother Who Killed Her Child," had been published in an 1856 issue of *The American Baptist*.

The report told how the slave, Margaret Garner, escaped with her four children to Ohio in 1851. But slave catchers soon tracked them down. The newspaper story described the mother's actions: "She caught a shovel and struck two of her children on the head, and then took a knife and cut the throat of the third, and tried to kill the other." Garner is quoted as saying she "would much rather kill them at once, and thus end their sufferings, than have them taken back to slavery, and be murdered by piecemeal."

The escaped slave did not go to trial for trying to kill her children. The court charged Garner for what it saw as the real crime—running away.

On reading Garner's story, Toni tried to understand the slave's sorrow—"a despair quite new to me but so deep it had no passion at all and elicited no tears." These emotions settled deeply into Toni's consciousness, gradually emerging as a novel about slavery and its destructive effect on African-American families. It took Toni three years to absorb the essence of her characters, understand the events they lived through, and research slavery, including taking a trip to Brazil to study devices used to control slaves. The process of developing the ideas for the novel took a long time. As she explained, before she began the story, "I was still at work, though I hadn't put a word down." The actual writing took another three years.

Before she could write the slave mother's story, Toni had to get inside the woman's mind and soul. She found the experience frightening and totally consuming. She noted later that it was good she did not have regular office hours at the time. Entering the mind of a slave who had killed her children caused Toni such emotional turmoil that she would have been useless in a modern business office. "I used to go into a space—a world of writing—and it was so vivid," she remembered with a shudder. "That goes on for months. And you worry that you're not going to come back up."

The result of this difficult experience was *Beloved,* which was dedicated to the 60 million Africans who died as a result of slavery. *Beloved* does not retell Margaret Garner's story, but the novel was inspired by the event. The main character in Morrison's book is a former slave named Sethe, who must cope with having killed her daughter, referred to as "Beloved." Sethe is haunted by the ghost of Beloved for years, until her old friend Paul D., another former slave, arrives and appears to successfully cast out the baby's spirit. But one day a 20-year-old stranger with a scar on her throat arrives at the door of Sethe's home. The young woman cannot explain where she came from and simply calls herself Beloved. She proceeds to nearly destroy Sethe until a group of former slave women are able to exorcise the spirit of Beloved.

The book takes place in the North, several years after the Civil War and the end of slavery. The story is more about the memory of slavery than the experience, although there are flashbacks to pre-Civil War South; *Beloved* explores how some African Americans are haunted by the painful legacy of slavery. It's about how individuals learn to deal with life while wrestling with the actions and memories of the past.

In an interview with the *Los Angeles Times,* Morrison explained how she wrote *Beloved* to understand the emotional, the human response to slavery. "I certainly thought I knew as much about slavery as anybody," Morrison said, "But it was the interior life I needed to find out about."

Published in 1987, *Beloved* received laudatory reviews. John Leonard wrote in the *Los Angeles Times Book Review* that *Beloved* "belongs on the highest shelf

Toni poses with her fifth novel, Beloved, *in September 1987, shortly after the book's release.*

of American literature, even if half a dozen canonized white boys have to be elbowed off. . . . Without *Beloved* our imagination of the nation's self has a hole in it big enough to die from."

Many other critics shared Leonard's passion about *Beloved,* and a number of novelists praised the work as well. However, the vocal support of her peers was about to place Toni Morrison in the center of controversy.

The popularity and exceptional quality of her novels earned Toni Morrison recognition throughout the world, and her engagement calendar was soon filled with lectures and book readings.

7

EARNING RECOGNITION

oni Morrison's fans eagerly waited to hear that *Beloved* would be awarded a major literary prize, perhaps a National Book Award or National Book Critics Circle Award. But the prizes went elsewhere. Disturbed by the lack of recognition for what they regarded as truly fine literature, 48 African-American authors signed a letter, published in the *New York Times Book Review* on January 24, 1988, complaining that a great black author was being ignored.

The action was badly timed. Just a few weeks later Toni was awarded the 1988 Pulitzer Prize in fiction, and the honor appeared to have been given in response to the *New York Times* statement. Although the Pulitzer judges announced that the protest had had no effect on their decision, the controversy tainted the honorary recognition. In explaining why he signed the letter, critic John Leonard later wrote, "All of us took *Beloved* personally; its career in the world mattered more to us than our own, like a favorite child."

Not all African-American critics and writers support Toni Morrison's books as enthusiastically. Some criticize her for not doing more to support black nationalism, a movement that emphasizes the importance of maintaining a strong racial identity and glorifying the African past through literary and artistic expression. Black nationalists maintain that African identity is important for black people all over the world, no matter how far removed they may be from their original African roots. In the United States, many black nationalists believe that African Americans should fight against being incorporated into white society, and instead build their own separate community in America.

A popular phrase that grew out of black nationalism is "Black is beautiful." Toni regarded this slogan as "an accurate but wholly irrelevant observation if ever there was one." In her view, the mere fact that some African Americans believed that the slogan was necessary showed how white-oriented African Americans were.

A number of African Americans do believe in the value of building a black culture separate from that of whites. This movement, known as the *black aesthetic*, supports the exploration of black history by reclaiming the past through literature and art. The creation of black studies departments at many universities was an outgrowth of this movement. These departments remain as centers of African-American or Afro-American studies today.

As much as she agreed with many black nationalist attitudes, Toni did not write to support the goals of black nationalism. However, much of her work seems to reflect the goals of the black aesthetic movement. Still, her tales can help educate both black and white people about black history.

In the 1970s members of the growing women's liberation movement also judged Toni Morrison's writing. Few African-American women took any significant part in the movement because, while many white women were seeking jobs outside the home as a matter of choice,

most black women had already been working outside the home to insure their family's economic survival. Toni was deeply aware of how the attitudes of black and white women differed. She told one interviewer:

> There is something inside [black women] that makes us different from other people. It is not like men and it is not like white women. . . . I don't have to make choices about whether to be a mother or whether to work. I do them both because they both exist and I don't feel put out about it. I don't dwell on the idea that I am a full human being. I know that.

Before Toni Morrison gained success with her writing, black women writers received little recognition.

The academic world has honored both Morrison's writing and teaching. Columbia University recognized her accomplishments with an award presented by school president Michael I. Sovern in 1988.

Morrison once noted:

> [N]o women writers were taken seriously. . . . Writing is a formidable thing to break into for anybody. For most black women in the past there was no time to write. . . . [Black women] seem to be the only people writing who do not regard white men and white women—the white world—as being at center stage. White men write about white men, because that's who they are; white women are interested in white men because they are their fathers, lovers and children, family; black men are interested in white men because that's the area in which they make the confrontation. . . . Black women don't seem to be interested in this confrontation.

Many people believe that Morrison creates much stronger women characters than men in her novels, but Toni considers such views a reflection of people's low expectations for women in the first place. Growing up, Toni was surrounded by strong, confident women— her mother, her grandmother, and her older sister. They all expected her to be just as strong and assertive as they were. "It never occurred to me that that was a feminist activity," she said.

Perhaps as a result of her own experiences, Toni also does not accept the notion that a single woman heading a household is a problem, or that a family in such a situation is "broken." She has attributed such views to beliefs "that a woman—and I have raised two children, alone—is somehow lesser than a male head. Or that I am incomplete without the male. This is not true."

In the university setting, Morrison's interest in women's issues have contributed to her desire to teach courses on black women writers, usually to female students. In most other literature courses, students could go to what are called secondary sources—information about the writers and their books. But for a course on black women writers, few secondary sources exist. The students themselves have to critique these writers.

Morrison notes: "One thing that has interested me is how enormously timid the students are about risking any criticism on things where there are only primary sources. . . . They are really unwilling to pass judgment on paper about a book that has only a few little reviews to examine."

She observes that in general women have not had much practice on passing intellectual judgment, and that much that has been written about women writers has been distorted.

Toni also teachers her students how to study writing. When teaching black literature, she discusses how black women writers portray black women as real people, rather than as the stereotypical figures often created by male writers. She also examines how fictional characters are developed. She presents the idea that characters should not be created just to serve a specific purpose and time. The broader treatment she deems important is apparent in her own work: she gives each of her characters a background—ancestors, a home, hobbies, religion, and family relationships. Many of her characters have connections to the South, even if they don't actually live in one of the southern states.

As Toni Morrison was teaching courses on topics such as "Black Women and Contemporary Literature," her books were becoming the subject of numerous college literature courses. In 1988, poet Nikki Giovanni, working at Virginia Tech University, taught the first class in the nation devoted entirely to Toni Morrison's books. Giovanni had been inspired by Toni's work when she read the author's first novel, *The Bluest Eye*. The poet immediately recognized that Morrison was special, capable of speaking with "the voice of a black woman," and in a way that included all readers.

In 1989 Morrison left SUNY at Albany to teach at Princeton University, where she had been named the Robert F. Goheen Professor in the Council of the Humanities. This made her the first African-American

*In 1987 Toni was named the
Robert F. Goheen Professor in
the Council of the Humanities
at Princeton University (above).
When she assumed the position
in 1989, she became the first
African-American woman
to hold an endowed chair
professorship at an Ivy
League university.*

woman writer to hold a chair position at an Ivy
League university. Of her decision to accept the professorship, Toni said, "I take teaching as seriously as I do
my writing." At Princeton Morrison holds appoint-
ments in the departments of creative writing and
African-American studies.

Toni continues to embrace new opportunities. In
the early 1990s, the management of Carnegie Hall,
the famous concert hall in New York City, asked Toni
to write the lyrics for a series—or cycle—of songs
to celebrate the hall's 100th anniversary. American
symphony conductor and composer André Previn

composed the music, which was performed by the renowned African-American soprano Kathleen Battle. The result of their combined efforts was the short work *Honey and Rue,* which debuted in 1992. A review in *Gramophone Magazine* noted that "Toni Morrison's words and André Previn's music sound as if they found each other a long time ago."

But in the midst of her widening opportunities, Toni never stopped writing. Although she did not see her fiction as an avenue for advocating particular social changes, she did write about social causes that concerned her. One such event occurred in 1991 when Clarence Thomas was nominated by President George Bush to be a justice of the U.S. Supreme Court. The U.S. Senate has to confirm such nominations, and during hearings on Thomas, a black lawyer named Anita Hill asked to testify.

All America watched the television broadcasts of the Senate hearings, which showed the black woman who had been Thomas's aide accuse him of sexual harassment and attempted seduction. Clarence Thomas flatly denied all charges and after weeks of controversial hearings, the Senate approved his nomination as a Supreme Court justice by the close margin of 52 to 48.

Disturbed by the controversy, Toni Morrison compiled and edited a collection of essays about the spectacle. *Race-ing Justice, En-gendering Power: Essays on Anita Hill, Clarence Thomas, and the Construction of Social Reality* was published a year later.

Speaking out on important issues did not cause Toni to neglect her fiction writing. The inspiration for her sixth novel, *Jazz,* came from seeing an unusual photograph. It was in *The Harlem Book of the Dead,* a collection of 1920s photographs of families' deceased loved ones taken by photographer James Van Der Zee. Morrison found her attention caught by the picture of a young girl in a coffin. The caption

The controversial U.S. Senate confirmation hearings on the nomination of Clarence Thomas as a justice of the U.S. Supreme Court led Toni Morrison to compile and edit a collection of essays about the incident.

explained the 18-year-old girl had been dancing at a party when she suddenly slumped to the floor. She had been shot by a jealous ex-boyfriend but would not accuse him; instead she gave him time to get away, and died shortly thereafter.

In describing this inspiration for her next novel, *Jazz*, Toni explained that she thought the story had "that quality of romance, misguided but certainly intense, that seems to feed into the music of that period."

Published in 1992, *Jazz* was Toni's first novel set in a big city. The author knew that African Americans who had migrated to cities faced choices that they would not have had in the South. "I wanted this young girl to have heard all that music, all the speakeasy music, and to be young and in the city and alive and daring and rebellious and, naturally, to get in trouble."

In *Jazz*, trouble comes to 18-year-old Dorcas in the form of Joe Trace, a married, door-to-door salesman in his 50s. The two have a tempestuous affair which ends after three months when Dorcas leaves Joe for a younger man. In response Joe shoots and kills Dorcas. Joe's wife, Violet, appears uninvited at the funeral and tries to disfigure the dead girl's face with a butcher knife. The novel gets its name not only because it is set during the Jazz Age of the 1920s, but also because the narrative

The urban experience of young African Americans in the Jazz Age of the 1920s contributed to the ideas behind Morrison's sixth novel, Jazz.

follows the improvisational style of jazz music.

Morrison later described the relevance of jazz music to her book in this way: "One person doesn't dominate the whole performance—or if he or she does, he or she will have to take close, close notice of what another voice or instrument is doing or

When Jazz *hit the* New York Times *best-seller list, it was joined by two other novels written by African-American women. One of those books was* Possessing the Secret of Joy *by Alice Walker.*

saying, and listening to the other voice may, and frequently does, affect or alter what the other voices might do or say."

In the book, as in a piece of jazz music, different characters take over periodically and view the incidents from a different perspective. Even the narrator of the story has a restricted point of view, unlike the omniscient narrator who is aware of the entire action of a novel.

When *Jazz* hit the *New York Times* best-seller list, it was joined by two other novels written by African-American women. Never before had books by three black women appeared on the prestigious list at the same time. The two other books were Terry McMillan's *Waiting to Exhale* and Alice Walker's *Possessing the Secret of Joy.* At the same time Toni Morrison's book of essays, *Playing in the Dark: Whiteness and the Literary Imagination,* appeared on the nonfiction list. That in itself was a great accomplishment as books of literary criticism rarely appear on any best-seller list.

Morrison had first presented the essays of *Playing in the Dark* as a series of lectures at Harvard University. In them, she argues that in much literature an assumption is made that the reader is white, that "American" means "white." In her essays, she writes that the study of American literature should not marginalize the black presence. She calls for a reexamination of how the language and culture of black Americans have contributed to the development of the nation's literature. Also included in the collection is an analysis of the relative importance of black characters in the works of such writers as Willa Cather, Edgar Allan Poe, Mark Twain, and Ernest Hemingway.

For several years, Toni's novels themselves were the subject of intense study by literary scholars and college classes. Early in 1993, she received word that a new organization, the Toni Morrison Society, had been founded to study and promote her works. The society's headquarters were established at Georgia State University in Atlanta.

More recognition was to come. On April 24, 1995, the mayor of Atlanta declared April 24 as Toni Morrison Day. Speaking at that special occasion, Toni noted with justifiable pride that in focusing on the work of an African-American woman writer, society was finally recognizing a body of work that "just thirty years ago would not have gotten this kind of validation."

Waiting to Exhale *by Terry McMillan also appeared on the* New York Times *bestseller list with* Jazz *in 1992. Never before had books by three black women made the list at the same time.*

Toni Morrison poses outside her Princeton University office on October 7, 1993, shortly after learning she had won the Nobel Prize for Literature.

8

STILL BREAKING GROUND

arly one October morning in 1993, the incessant ringing of the telephone shook Toni awake. On the other end of the line was a friend at Princeton University, calling to relay what she had just heard on the news: Toni had been named the Nobel laureate in literature.

Morrison had always assumed that writers chosen for the Nobel Prize were those who wrote about the universal condition of human beings. And as she later explained in an interview, she didn't see her books as indicative of any "condition," either specifically black or generally human. She viewed her novels as stories about very specific individuals in very specific circumstances.

Many critics disagree with this assessment, however. They praise Morrison's ability to provide insight into the problems of all human beings. In the *Washington Post Book World*, Jonathan Yardley described Toni's writing: "Quite purposefully, it seems, she is striving not for the particular but for the universal." The Swedish Academy explained its choice of Toni for the Nobel Prize: "In novels characterized by visionary force and poetic import,

[she] gives life to an essential aspect of American reality."

An article in the *Journal of Gender Studies* examined the headlines and articles that appeared after Toni's selection was announced. It noted that when the Nobel Prize winner was announced, headlines included "eye-catching combinations of four words that do not often appear in the same sentence: 'winner,' 'black,' 'Nobel prize,' and 'woman.'" The article also observed that many journalists felt a need to defend her selection. "In rather crude terms, *The* [London] *Times* states that there are 'certainly strong reasons for suspecting that non-literary factors played a part in this unexpected decision,' though it concedes that Morrison 'has kept herself aloof from the more absurd follies of the race and gender lobbies.'"

Toni refused to let such comments keep her from enjoying herself during the Nobel Prize activities in early December. She believed that receiving the award was a great honor, one that symbolized long overdue recognition of women and black writers: "I felt I represented a whole world of women who either were silenced or who had never received the [stamp of approval] of the established literary world," she said.

She also saw her award as a symbol of hope for young black people. "Seeing me up there might encourage them to write one of those books I'm desperate to read. And *that* made me happy. It gave me license to strut," she declared.

But the joys of being honored with such a distinguished award were quickly overshadowed. On Christmas Day her house on the Hudson River burned down. "I regard the fact that my house burned down after I won the Nobel Prize," she dryly observed, "to be better than having my house burn down without having won the Nobel Prize. Most people's houses just burn down. Period."

She feared that she might not get over the event.

Toni Morrison relaxes in her New York City apartment, one of three homes she enjoys. The painting is a portrait made of her when she was 23.

Losing the furniture and appliances did not matter, but the loss of irreplaceable items such as family mementos, photographs, personal papers, and some original manuscripts of published works was wrenching. Many of the papers she had stored at her house were destroyed, some of which might have otherwise ended up in a university library. Fortunately, her works-in-progress were kept elsewhere and were not burned in the fire.

Soon after the shock of the Christmas Day fire came yet another loss. On February 17, 1994, Toni's mother, Ramah Willis Wofford, died in Elyria, Ohio. A small comfort to Toni was knowing that the woman who was so confident of her abilities had lived to learn that Toni had won the Nobel Prize for Literature.

Winning the Nobel Prize gave Toni even more opportunities. Always popular as a speaker, Toni received additional invitations to address commencements, writers conferences, and other gatherings. She became known for arriving late to functions simply because she had accepted too many invitations to fit in her schedule.

Despite the demands on Toni's time, she still concentrated as much as she could on her own writing and rewriting. She once told a Kansas City audience that she regards editing her own work as the most important thing she does. "It's the crafting and shaping of the language I enjoy most," she explained. Such attention to detail is vital to her as a writer. "There's a difference between writing for a living and writing for life," she said. "If you write for a living, you make enormous compromises, and you might not ever be able to uncompromise yourself. If you write for life, you'll work hard; you'll do it in a disciplined fashion; you'll do what's honest, not what pays."

Like most writers, Toni reads the works of other people to relax. However, when she's working on a novel, she can't read books by authors who write in a similar vein for fear that their phrases and ideas may end up in her writing. Instead, she'll immerse herself in detective stories such as those by Ruth Rendell and P. D. James, two favorite English women mystery writers. She also finds working in her garden both relaxing and challenging. She admits to watching television after a day of teaching and follows soap operas and Court TV. She frequently calls author/humorist Fran Lebowitz, one of her best friends, to discuss what they're watching on TV.

Morrison's professional responsibilities have not kept her from developing a rich and varied personal life. Over the years, she has developed many close friendships with both black and white people. In 1994 poet and writer Maya Angelou held a dinner for Toni Morrison and poet Rita Dove, who was at the time the poet laureate of the United States. Angelou didn't

simply host the dinner at her home in Winston-Salem, North Carolina; she also cooked the entire meal for her 150 guests. Among those attending were television host Oprah Winfrey, political activist Angela Davis, and opera singer Jessye Norman.

Toni continues to keep public knowledge of her personal life to a minimum. Other than the bare facts of places and dates that are a matter of public record, most information about her is derived from reading her books and interpreting what she says in interviews. She once summed up her life in an interview with Claudia Dreifus: "I'm not pleased with all the events and accidents of my life. You know, life is pretty terrible and some of it has hurt me a lot. I'd say I'm proud of a third of my life, comfortable with another third and would like to redo, reconfigure, the last third." She later added, "Being able to laugh got me through."

Distinguished poet Maya Angelou cooks at her home in Winston-Salem, North Carolina. In 1994, Angelou hosted and prepared a dinner for 150 guests that honored Toni Morrison and poet Rita Dove.

Morrison's two sons, now grown, are a significant part of the third of her life that brings her pride. Ford is a musician and a sound engineer, and Slade is an architect, like his father. Toni remains intimately involved in the lives of her other relatives, and she visits them as often as possible, especially her sister Lois in Ohio.

Toni maintains several homes—in New York City; in Rockland County, New York; and near Princeton, New Jersey—a fact that some observers have attributed to her childhood fear of being evicted. She is rebuilding the Hudson River boathouse, but usually spends most of her time in Princeton.

The fact that she can maintain several homes is due, of course, to the financial success of her writing. She briefly discussed this subject with *Essence* magazine editors in an interview published in May 1995, transforming an intimate discussion into an observation on the human condition: "Capitalism feels good. Money feels good. Houses feel good. All that feels good, and it can be a complete substitution for being good." Then she told the editors, "Recently two close cousins died, both of my brothers died, my mother died, my house burned down. Sometimes things are in disarray, My faith is always being challenged, but that is good: You discover of what you are made."

Another honor came to Toni in 1996 when she was chosen by the National Council on the Humanities to deliver the Jefferson Lecture in the Humanities at the Kennedy Center in Washington, D.C. Being chosen to deliver this lecture, which has been given annually since 1972, is the highest honor for intellectual achievement in the humanities that the federal government awards. Others who have been named Jefferson Lecturers include African-American poet Gwendolyn Brooks, Nobel Prize novelist Saul Bellow, and literary critic Lionel Trilling.

On March 25, 1996, Toni gave the Jefferson Lecture. She spoke before a filled auditorium on the subject

"The Future of Time: Literature and Diminished Expectations." She argued that the purpose of literature was to give modern society the power to imagine the future. "Literature, sensitive as a tuning fork, is an unblinking witness to the light and shade of the world we live in," she said.

That same year, she compiled a collection of essays in response to the O. J. Simpson murder trial. In January 1995 former football star O. J. Simpson, an African American, went on trial for the murders of his white ex-wife, Nicole Brown Simpson, and her friend Ronald Goldman. Coverage of the event lasted for months, and the case brought fame and notoriety to almost anyone associated with Simpson. In October of that same year, the jury acquitted Simpson. The not-guilty verdict polarized blacks and whites in the United States as most African Americans considered Simpson innocent of the crime, while a majority of whites believed him guilty. In response Morrison compiled and edited a collection of essays entitled *Birth of a Nation'hood: Gaze, Script, and Spectacle in the O. J. Simpson Case,* which offers social commentary on the racial attitudes raised by the tragic events.

In the fall of 1996, television talk-show host Oprah Winfrey began an on-air book club to publicize novels she thinks worthy of more readers. The club has had a remarkable effect on book publishing. Each book Oprah Winfrey has featured on her book club list has sold thousands more copies than its publisher expected. Oprah chose Toni Morrison's *Song of Solomon* as the second book discussed on the program, one of the few selections that was not a recently released title. After being featured on Oprah Winfrey's book list, the novel sold more copies in three months than it had during its entire 20-year history.

Winfrey's interest in Toni Morrison's writing extended beyond *Song of Solomon*. The moment the host had read *Beloved* in 1987, she'd felt a great kinship with the main character, Sethe, and decided that she

After Toni Morrison appeared on The Oprah Winfrey Show *to discuss her novel* Song of Solomon, *the book sold more copies during the next three months than it had during its previous 20-year history.*

wanted to make a film version of the novel. She called Morrison on the phone and asked to purchase the book's movie rights.

Toni had previously decided that her books would lose much of their character if turned into movies. However, when Oprah Winfrey asked for the rights to *Beloved,* the author reconsidered her position.

Morrison later recalled her conversation with Winfrey:

> She said, and this is kind of charming, "I am going in my pocketbook and write a check." I wasn't talking to a studio or a lawyer but to another human being. If you'll excuse it, it reminded me of myself. A single black woman who said, "Well, I'm doing this. It's going to be hard for me, but that's beside the point." This was a big project and, for her, a big deal. And she was deadly serious about every aspect of it.

After obtaining the movie rights, Winfrey took several years to prepare to make the film. Because the book is structured so that present and past—and living and dead—intermingle, the screenplay was difficult to create. Winfrey's film version of *Beloved,* released in 1998, closely follows the story line of the book. "Almost everything, every line of dialogue, every article of clothing, every detail we shamelessly took from the book to put in the movie," said director Jonathan Demme. "If Toni Morrison said black dress, it was going to be a black dress."

Ultimately, Toni was pleased with the results, observing, "They did something I thought they never could: to make the film represent not the abstraction of slavery but the individuals, the domestic qualities and consequences of it."

Danny Glover and Oprah Winfrey portray Paul D. and Sethe in a scene from the film version of Beloved.

While Oprah Winfrey was busy bringing *Beloved* to the screen, its author was working on her next novel, *Paradise*. The story begins with one of Morrison's most riviting opening lines: "They shoot the white girl first." From that violent start, *Paradise* flashes back to the tale of an all-black town in Oklahoma founded by former slaves. Their descendants—feeling threatened as other people begin to settle nearby—move the town, change its name, and gradually form a male-dominated society. Feeling their dominance threatened by four women who live in a nearby convent, the men turn the women into scapegoats for the community's ills and decide to massacre them, starting with the white girl.

But the reader does not know which of the four women is the white girl. Anna Mulrine of *U.S. News and World Report* described Toni Morrison's technique as "a bold literary device: In struggling to figure out which of the women is white, the reader is forced to ask why that detail even matters." Toni explained in an interview that "race is the least reliable information you can have about someone. It's real information, but it tells you next to nothing."

Paradise received mixed reviews. Geoffrey Bent wrote, "Though Morrison doesn't run the risk of having her prize reclaimed by Stockholm, this book can only send ripples of reappraisal back over the rest of her oeuvre." Other reviewers, though, agreed with critic John Leonard, who thought the book added to the author's stature as "the best writer in America."

Oprah Winfrey chose *Paradise* for inclusion in her book club. Knowing that many readers in her audience would find the book difficult to read because the story does not follow a chronological order, Winfrey invited a group of women to interview Toni in the writer's Princeton office. During the session one of the women asked, "Are we supposed to get it on the first read?" Toni replied that she doesn't expect people to "read it to the bone" the first time.

No matter what Toni Morrison does, people sit up and take notice. In 1999 she published a well-received book of verse for children. Created 20 years before with her son Slade, *The Big Box* is an illustrated story about three rowdy children whose parents, thinking the children cannot handle freedom, keep them in a large box filled with toys and pictures and games. The children possess many things but have no freedom to explore and create.

In an interview with *People* magazine, Toni explained the book's message: "It's so much easier to provide things for the happiness and care of our children. It's much harder to be imaginative, to listen or have conversations in which the parent is vulnerable." Having released one successful children's book, Toni is committed to completing more titles for young fans. She started with *The Book of Mean People*, published in 2001 by Disney Press.

In 2000, Toni made another mark on the literary scene when she became the first writer to have three of her books promoted on three different shows of Oprah's Book Club. Thirty years after its publication, *The Bluest Eye*, Toni's first novel, received recognition with its inclusion on the book club list.

As the Swedish Academy once observed, Toni Morrison remains most famous for her compelling and poetic use of language. Critic Carolyn Denard noted, "In a world where language is taken-for-granted, limited and abused, destructive and despairing, [Toni Morrison] restores for us the good, transformative qualities of language—its wonder, its power, and its magic." Toni herself said, "I try to clean up the language and give words back their original meaning, not the one that's sabotaged by constant use." She delights in being satisfied with her writing. "When the language fits and it's graceful and powerful and like what I've always remembered black people's language to be, I'm

Among the causes that Toni supports is the education of writers. On November 16, 1997, she appeared at a Borders bookstore in New York City, where Tim Hopkins (left) of Borders presented a book sales donation of $15,000 to Neil Baldwin (center) of the National Book Foundation. The money was used to sponsor adult students at the foundation's Summer Writing Camp.

ecstatic," she told Mel Watkins of the *New York Times*.

Toni counts on language to draw readers into her books so that they can participate in her stories, instead of just reading the words. "In the same way when a preacher delivers a sermon he really expects his congregation to listen, participate, approve, disapprove, and interject almost as much as he does. Eventually, I think, if the life of the novels is long, then the readers who wish to read my books will know that it is not I who do it, it is they who do."

Each time Toni Morrison finishes writing a book, she goes through a period of loneliness. "I feel something's missing," she has said. "I miss the characters, their company, the sense of possibility in them." Never having been able to work on more than one book at a time, she is forced to wait for the next idea. "[It's] as though I've lost touch, though momentarily, with some collective memory." But then an image comes—usually the end of a story comes first. It begins to percolate in her imagination, and she begins scratching notes on her yellow legal pad, delving into the world of another set of fascinating characters. Early in her writing life, Toni told an interviewer, "The next book will have different hurdles. Whatever it is, it'll be different from the last one. But they will always be about the same thing—you know—about the whole world of Black people in this country."

That world was not represented in the books available to Morrison as a child, but she remains committed to giving it a voice in American literature. A student at Princeton University once asked Toni whom she wrote for. "I want to write for people like me," she replied, "which is to say black people, curious people, demanding people—people who can't be faked, people who don't need to be patronized, people who have very, very high criteria." Never satisfied by what she has already accomplished, Toni Morrison continues to challenge herself with "very, very high criteria" in her quest to translate the world of her imagination to paper.

CHRONOLOGY

1931   Born Chloe Anthony Wofford on February 18 in Lorain, Ohio, the second of four children of Ramah Willis and George Wofford

1949   Graduates with honors from Lorain High School; enters Howard University, Washington, D.C.; changes name to Toni

1953   Graduates with B.A. in English from Howard University; enters Cornell University, New York, for graduate studies in English

1955   Receives M.A. in English from Cornell University; becomes instructor in English at Texas Southern University, Houston

1957   Returns to Howard University as instructor in English

1958   Marries Jamaican architect Harold Morrison

1961   Son, Harold Ford, is born

1962   Joins a writers group

1964   Resigns from Howard University; divorces Harold Morrison; returns to her parents' home in Lorain, Ohio; second son, Slade Kevin, is born

1965   Moves to Syracuse, New York, to work as editor for L. W. Singer Publishing Company, a textbook subsidiary of Random House

1967   Transfers to New York City and is promoted to senior editor at Random House

1970   First novel, *The Bluest Eye,* is published

1971   Becomes associate professor of English at the State University of New York (SUNY) at Purchase

1973   Second novel, *Sula,* is published

1974   *The Black Book,* a Random House project Toni helped develop, is published

1975   *Sula* is nominated for the National Book Award

1976   Becomes a visiting lecturer at Yale University

1977   Third novel, *Song of Solomon,* is published and is chosen as a main selection of the Book-of-the-Month Club; Morrison receives the National Book Critics Circle Award for *Song of Solomon*; is appointed to National Council of the Arts by President Jimmy Carter

1978   *Writers in America,* a PBS television series, devotes an entire segment to exploring Toni Morrison's writing

1981   Fourth novel, *Tar Baby,* is published; Morrison appears on the cover of *Newsweek* magazine and is elected to the American Academy and Institute of Arts and Letters

1984   Leaves Random House; accepts appointment to the Albert
        Schweitzer Chair in the Humanities at SUNY Albany

1986   *Dreaming Emmett* premiers at the Marketplace Capitol Repertory
        Theater of Albany, New York, on January 4

1987   Fifth novel, *Beloved*, is published to great acclaim; the novel is
        nominated for a National Book Award and a National Book
        Critics Circle Award and is the main selection of the Book-of-
        the-Month Club

1988   Morrison receives Pulitzer Prize in fiction for *Beloved*

1989   Appointed the Robert F. Goheen Professor in the Humanities at
        Princeton University, becoming the first black woman to have an
        endowed chair at an Ivy League university

1992   *Honey and Rue* premiers at Carnegie Hall in New York City with lyrics
        by Toni; sixth novel, *Jazz*, and essay compilation *Playing in the Dark:
        Whiteness and the Literary Imagination* published; both books appear
        on the *New York Times* best-seller lists; edits and writes introduction
        to *Race-ing Justice, En-gendering Power: Essays on Anita Hill,
        Clarence Thomas, and the Construction of Social Reality*

1993   Toni Morrison Society founded at Georgia State University, Atlanta,
        Georgia; Morrison receives Nobel Prize in Literature; home near
        Nyack, New York, burns

1996   Morrison chosen to deliver the Jefferson Lecture by the National
        Council on the Humanities

1997   Publishes *Birth of a Nation'hood: Gaze, Script, and Spectacle in the
        O. J. Simpson Case*

1998   Film adaptation of *Beloved* (produced by Oprah Winfrey) released;
        Morrison's seventh novel, *Paradise*, is published

1999   *The Big Box*, a picture book in rhyme written jointly by Toni and her
        son Slade, is published

2001   *The Book of Mean People* scheduled for release

ACCOMPLISHMENTS

Books (Fiction)

1970　*The Bluest Eye*

1974　*Sula*

1977　*Song of Solomon*

1981　*Tar Baby*

1987　*Beloved*

1992　*Jazz*

1998　*Paradise*

1999　*The Big Box* (with Slade Morrison)

2001　*The Book of Mean People*

Books (Nonfiction)

1974　*The Black Book* (editor)

1992　*Playing in the Dark: Whiteness and the Literary Imagination*

　　　　Race-ing Justice, En-gendering Power: Essays on Anita Hill, Clarence Thomas, and the Construction of Social Reality (editor)

1994　*The Nobel Lecture in Literature*

1995　*To Die for the People: The Writings of Huey P. Newton* (editor)

1997　*Birth of a Nation'hood : Gaze, Script, and Spectacle in the O. J. Simpson Case* (edited with Claudia Brodsky Lacour)

Drama

1985　*Dreaming Emmett* (unpublished)

1992　*Honey and Rue* (lyrics)

Recordings

1994　*Toni Morrison: Lecture and Speech of Acceptance upon the Award of the Nobel Prize for Literature, Delivered in Stockholm on the Seventh of December*

1996　*The Dancing Mind: Speech upon Acceptance of the National Book Foundation Medal for Distinguished Contribution to American Letters on the Sixth of November*

BIBLIOGRAPHY

Books and Periodicals

Angelo, Bonnie. "The Pain of Being Black." *Time*, 22 May 1989.

Bent, Geoffrey. "Less Than Divine: Toni Morrison's Paradise." *Southern Review*, Winter 1999.

Brown, Cecil. "Interview with Toni Morrison." *Massachusetts Review: A Quarterly of Literature*, Autumn–Winter 1995.

Brown, Joseph A. "To Cheer the Weary Traveler: Toni Morrison, William Faulkner, and History." *Mississippi Quarterly*, February 1996.

Caldwell, Gail. "Morrison Awarded Nobel: Writer's 'Visionary Force' Cited." *Boston Globe*, 8 October 1993.

Cawley, Janet. "25 Most Powerful Women in America." *Biography*, April 1999.

Corliss, Richard, et al. "Bewitching Beloved." *Time*, 5 October 1998.

Denard, Carolyn. "Blacks, Modernism, and the American South: An Interview with Toni Morrison." *Studies in the Literary Imagination*, Fall 1998.

Dreifus, Claudia. "Chloe Wofford Toni Morrison." *New York Times Magazine*, 11 September 1994.

Dubey, Madhu. *Black Women Novelists and the Nationalist Aesthetic*. Indianapolis: Indiana Univ. Press, 1994.

Evans, Mari, ed. *Black Women Writers (1950-1980): A Critical Evaluation*. Garden City, N.Y.: Doubleday, 1984.

Fabi, M. Giulia. "On Nobel Prizes and the 'Robinson Crusoe Syndrome': The Case of Toni Morrison." *Journal of Gender Studies*, November 1993.

Gates Jr., Henry Louis, and K. A. Appiah, eds. *Toni Morrison: Critical Perspectives Past and Present*. New York: Amistad, 1993.

Gray, Paul. "Literature Rooms of Their Own: Toni Morrison." *Time*, 18 October 1993.

———. "Paradise Found." *Time*, 19 January 1998.

Hackney, Sheldon. "'I Come From People Who Sang All the Time': A Conversation with Toni Morrison." *Humanities*, March–April 1996.

Harris, Middleton. *The Black Book*. New York: Random House, 1974.

Holden-Kirwan, Jennifer L. "Looking into the Self That Is No Self: An Examination of Subjectivity in Beloved." *African American Review*, Fall 1998.

Holloway, Karla F. C., and Stephanie A. Demetrakopoulos. *New Dimensions of Spirituality: A Biracial and Bicultural Reading of the Novels of Toni Morrison*. Contributions in Women's Studies, no. 84. New York: Greenwood Press, 1987.

BIBLIOGRAPHY

Jaffrey, Zia. "Toni Morrison." *Salon,* 2 February 1998.

Kuenz, Jane. "The Bluest Eye: Notes on History, Community, and Black Female Subjectivity." *African American Review,* Fall 1993.

Leonard, John. "Her Soul's High Song." *Nation,* 25 May 1992.

———. "Shooting Women." *Nation,* 26 January 1998.

———. "Travels with Toni." *Nation,* 17 January 1994.

McDowell, Edwin. "Toni Morrison: Behind the Best Sellers." *New York Times,* 11 September 1977.

Mobley, Marilyn Sanders. "The Mellow Moods and Difficult Truths of Toni Morrison." *Southern Review,* Summer 1993.

Morrison, Toni. *In Black and White: Conversations with African-American Writers,* "Part 3: Toni Morrison." RTSI-Swiss Television, videocassette, 1992.

———. "Rediscovering Black History." *New York Times Magazine,* 11 August 1974.

———. "Rootedness: The Ancestor as Foundation." In *Black Women Writers (1950–1980): A Critical Evaluation.* Garden City, N.Y.: Anchor Books, 1984.

Mulrine, Anna. "This Side of 'Paradise.'" *U.S. News and World Report,* 19 January 1998.

Nigro, Marie. "In Search of Self: Frustration and Denial in Toni Morrison's *Sula.*" *Journal of Black Studies,* July 1998.

"Nobel Prize-Winning Author Toni Morrison Recalls What Her Father Taught Her About Racism." *Jet,* 31 August 1998.

Peach, Linden. *Toni Morrison.* St. Martin's, 1995.

Peterson, V. R. "Talking with . . . Toni Morrison." *People,* 1 November 1999.

Pinson, Hermine. "Paradise." *America.* 15 August 1998.

Plimpton, George, ed. *Women Writers at Work: The Paris Review.* New York: Random House, 1998.

Powell, Timothy B. "Toni Morrison: The Struggle to Depict the Black Figure on the White Page." *Black American Literature Forum,* Winter 1990.

Price, Reynolds. "Black Family Chronicle." *New York Times,* 11 September 1977.

Reilly, Joseph. "Under the White Gaze: Jim Crow, the Nobel, and the Assault on Toni Morrison." *Monthly Review,* April 1994.

"The Roots of 'Paradise.'" *Economist.* 6 June 1998.

Samuels, Wilfred D., and Clenora Hudson-Weems. *Toni Morrison.* Boston: Twayne Publishers, 1990.

Tate, Claudia, ed. *Black Women Writers at Work*. New York: Continuum, 1983.

Taylor-Guthrie, Danielle, ed. *Conversations with Toni Morrison*. Literary Conversations Series. Jackson, Miss.: Univ. Press of Mississippi, 1994.

"Teaching the Literature of Toni Morrison: The Focus of Princeton Conference." *Black Issues in Higher Education*. 4 March 1999.

The Dancing Mind: Speech upon Acceptance of the National Book Foundation Medal for Distinguished Contribution to American Letters on the Sixth of November. New York: Random House Audiobooks, 1996.

"Toni Morrison." *Current Biography Yearbook 1979*. New York: H. W. Wilson, 1979.

"Toni Morrison." *Time Australia*, 17 June 1996.

"Toni Morrison's Gift." *Boston Globe*, 8 October 1993.

Toni Morrison: Lecture and Speech of Acceptance, upon the Award of the Nobel Prize for Literature, Delivered in Stockholm on the Seventh of December. New York: Random House Audiobooks, 1994.

Toni Morrison Society Newsletter 2, no. 2 (1995).

Watkins, Mel. "Talk with Toni Morrison." *New York Times*, 11 September 1977.

Wilcots, Barbara J. "Toni Morrison's Folk Roots." *African American Review*, Winter 1992.

"The World According to Toni Morrison." *Essence*, May 1995.

Websites

http://www.penguinputnam.com/academic/resources/guides/morrison/content ("A Teacher's Guide to the Signet and Plume Edition of Toni Morrison's *Beloved*," by Elizabeth Ann Poe. Penguin Putnam.)

http://www.nobel.se/literature/laureates/1993/morrison-lecture ("Nobel Lecture," by Toni Morrison. Nobel Lectures.)

http://www.hwwilson.com ("Toni Morrison," *1997 Biography from Nobel Prize Winners 1992–1996*. H. W. Wilson Company.)

http://www.Africana.com ("Toni Morrison." Africana.)

http://www.bn.com ("Toni Morrison." Barnes & Noble Biography.)

http://www.galenet.com ("Toni Morrison." Contemporary Authors Online 1999. Gale.)

http://www.penguinputnam.com ("Toni Morrison Biography." Penguin Putnam.)

INDEX

INDEX

PICTURE CREDITS

Cover Photo: Micheline Pelletier/Corbis-Sygma

Jean F. Blashfield is the author of almost 100 books, many of them for young adults. Her writings have covered subjects such as women's history, foreign countries, murderers, science, World War II, and the American Civil War. She lives in Delavan, Wisconsin, and has a son in graduate school and a daughter in college. She would like to thank the women of the Bluestockings Book Group of the American Association of University Women Geneva Lake Branch for their support and enthusiastic assistance in writing this book.

Matina S. Horner was president of Radcliffe College and associate professor of psychology and social relations at Harvard University. She is best known for her studies of women's motivation, achievement, and personality development. Dr. Horner has served on several national boards and advisory councils, including those of the National Science Foundation, Time Inc., and the Women's Research and Education Institute. She earned her B.A. from Bryn Mawr College and her Ph.D. from the University of Michigan, and holds honorary degrees from many colleges and universities, including Mount Holyoke, Smith, Tufts, and the University of Pennsylvania.